DIGERATI GLITTERATI
High-Tech Heroes

Christopher Langdon and David Manners

*"I strongly commend Digerati Glitterati to all who are
interested in the IT revolution and its application to business. It
demonstrates very clearly the different approaches to business,
innovation and risk which are the foundations for success in
this new and ubiquitous world."*

SIR JOHN HARVEY-JONES

JOHN WILEY & SONS, LTD
Chichester · New York · Weinheim · Brisbane · Singapore · Toronto

Other Wiley Editorial Offices

John Wiley & Sons, Inc., 605 Third Avenue,
New York, NY 10158-0012, USA

WILEY-VCH GmbH, Pappelallee 3,
D-69469 Weinheim, Germany

John Wiley & Sons Australia Ltd, 33 Park Road, Milton
Queensland 4064, Australia

John Wiley & Sons (Asia) Pte Ltd, 2 Clementi Loop #02-01,
Jin Xing Distripark, Singapore 129809

John Wiley & Sons (Canada) Ltd, 22 Worcester Road,
Rexdale, Ontario M9W 1L1, Canada

British Library Cataloguing in Publication Data

A catalogue record for this book is available from the British Library

ISBN 0-471-49949-8

Typeset in Garamond
Printed and bound in Great Britain by Biddles Ltd, Guildford and King's Lynn.
This book is printed on acid-free paper responsibly manufactured from sustainable forestry, in which at least two trees are planted for each one used for paper production.

CONTENTS

For
Sash, Gem and Isabella
and
to the memory of Martin Brent

INTRODUCTION

The researchers win Nobel Prizes, the entrepreneurs are the leading scientists of their day and the salesmen have PhDs – such an industry is different to other industries.

The intellectual power of the chip industry is awesome – but so are the egos. To keep people working together productively requires a very individual style of management.

The co-founders of Fairchild Semiconductor and Intel, Gordon Moore and Robert Noyce, did more than anyone to foster the unique style of egalitarian industrial democracy which, spreading out from its birthplace in Silicon Valley, prevails today throughout the high-tech industry.

Employees are expected to buy into the company's goals, values and culture and, in return, get shares in the company. Hierarchies are flat, outward signs of status like reserved car parking places or fancy offices are anathema, responsibilities are devolved to the operational level.

It was revolutionary stuff in the 1950s, and in many industries it is still revolutionary but, in the intellect-driven chip industry, the mind-set which devised that system of personal responsibility and reward is mainstream.

The bosses of such companies are a special breed. They hold their positions more by consent of their employees than the decree of the board of directors. For instance Gordon Moore relates in his chapter how the first thing they did after he and his seven colleagues left Shockley Semiconductor to found Fairchild Semiconductor was to advertise in the *Wall Street Journal* for someone to act as their boss.

Similarly Robin Saxby recalls that, on being offered the job as CEO of ARM, he said he'd only accept if ARM's employees wanted him. He then went to their offices and asked them.

Andrew Rickman tells how he looked to the culture that Gordon Moore personifies when he was setting up Bookham Technology. Not finding any example of it in the UK, he set about establishing such a culture from scratch. To do so, he appointed Americans or managers with US experience, in the top jobs and got Jack Kilby, co-inventor of the chip, to sit on his board.

Dick Skipworth, as familiar with California as Oxfordshire, also looked to the US example when establishing Memec.

Visit these people at work and you will find no trappings of success. The offices of Dick Skipworth and Hermann Hauser, founder of Acorn, ARM and Virata, are as utilitarian as offices can be.

Gordon Moore worked in a cubicle. Respected as the industry's role model, he is one of the finest chemists of his generation, but is personally so modest and unassuming that it was said of him: "You could spend a week in his company without finding out who he is."

The culture they create around them is an engineer's culture where everything and everyone is up for questioning and challenge – whoever the challenger and the challenged may be.

"It's a culture where you can criticise your boss, where you can have different opinions, where you are loyal to your company and not to your boss", is how Ulrich Schumacher, Infineon's CEO, describes it.

In a science-based, performance-oriented, ferociously competitive industry, the important thing is to get it right, not to preserve the boss's ego. If you want to produce products that conform to the laws of physics – and if they don't, they won't work – then you can't have a company culture that allows the truth to be hedged. You can't lie about Ohm's Law.

A brutal honesty is required if a chip company is to come up with the right solutions to engineering problems. Without a culture that consistently produces the right solutions, a company is soon overtaken by its competitors. "We hear footsteps behind us all the time," says Gordon Moore.

It is a culture that many high-tech entrepreneurs seek to preserve by investing in other would-be entrepreneurs. Gordon Moore's practice of investing in many other Silicon Valley start-up companies, besides the ones he founded, is a model for many of the UK entrepreneurs who see the importance of the genealogy of the entrepreneurial process.

Andrew Rickman, Hermann Hauser, Robin Saxby and Malcolm Miller of Pace Micro Technology, all talk about the importance of using the wealth created by one generation of entrepreneurs to fund the entrepreneurial ventures of a new generation.

Hermann Hauser points out how the success of ARM created 200 millionaires in the Cambridge area and Virata's success created another 100. All

300 represent a pool of wealth in the hands of informed, experienced, potential investors for repeating the virtuous circle of investment creating entrepreneurial success, which creates wealth that then goes into new investment.

As Silicon Valley has shown, there is nothing so effective as the collective judgement of a pool of independent investors for creating entrepreneurial success. Hermann Hauser's venture capital group in Cambridge, called Amadeus, is the UK embodiment of the Silicon Valley virtuous circle.

There's another aspect to the genealogy of entrepreneurship – success seeds success. Five of the *Digerati* in this book have close causal connections: for instance, the first products which David Potter at Psion produced were software for Sinclair's computers; Sinclair's chief salesman, Chris Curry, co-founded Acorn Computers with Hermann Hauser – copying Sinclair's business model; out of Acorn, came ARM – spun-off initially as a subsidiary headed up by Robin Saxby; also from Acorn came the technology originally used by Malcolm Miller's Pace Micro Technology for its set-top boxes; finally from the success of Acorn and ARM came the venture capital fund Amadeus which is funding a new generation of UK entrepreneurial high-tech companies like Element 14, sold in 2000 for $1 billion.

One of the reasons why European *Digerati* tend to be fervent on the subject of stock options – often illegal, restricted or heavily taxed in Europe – is because, without them, engineers will not be able to accumulate the wealth to become investors for the next generation of entrepreneurs.

The wish to perpetuate a high-tech entrepreneurial culture demonstrates another quality of the *Digerati* – their personal commitment to their companies. While CEOs in other industries parachute in, and scuttle away after they've cashed in their share options, these engineer-CEOs are team players.

Hermann Hauser tells how, in the early days at Acorn, he'd buy dinner for anyone who was still working after 8pm. These dinners were always at the same Italian restaurant near the market in Cambridge. Out of the dinners came many design ideas, product strategies and technological breakthroughs. But the main benefit was the team building.

Similarly, Ulrich Schumacher of Infineon Technologies, in his early days as a CEO, spent every workday evening for two years with colleagues in an Italian restaurant in Munich. "It was psychologically mandatory to cope with the pressure and the stress," he says.

For people who know they're working on the edge, success becomes an all-consuming passion, the excitement of the industry enters their bloodstream, and they're addicted.

"The only sane strategy is to bet the company regularly," says Gordon Moore. That keeps the temperature stoked up, the adrenaline flowing and the commitment intense. Even after relinquishing their executive roles, few walk away with their, very often substantial, rewards in order to sit on a beach. Being a business angel or a venture capitalist keeps them connected, gives them their fix.

What makes a *Digerati Glitterati*? Many date their interest in technology back to an early childhood experience. For Sir Clive Sinclair it was seeing an inventor on TV; for Gordon Moore it was when the boy next door got a chemistry set for Christmas; for Andrew Rickman it was buying a Sinclair amplifier kit, having trouble making it work, and getting a personal letter back from Sir Clive when he wrote to him about it; for both David Potter and Hermann Hauser it was go-karts; for Robin Saxby it was being given an electrical outfit "with valves, buzzers and batteries" at the age of eight. They all got hooked early on.

There's also a catalyst that turns the engineer into the CEO. David Potter lost his father at an early date and points out that the same is true about half the CEOs in the FTSE100, speculating that it breeds self-reliance and self-confidence; Pasquale Pistorio points to the pride and responsibility he learnt in helping his father as a boy; Robin Saxby sees his boyhood TV repair business as a key formative influence.

But it's more than that. These are people with very strong egos but with the intelligence to be able to suppress outward signs of ego in the interests of team building. David Potter and Hermann Hauser tell of how they fluttered around their design teams, making tea, bringing cakes, occasionally even offering advice. The *Digerati* CEO may have a big, maybe bigger, ego than anyone else in the team but he's figured out how to hide it.

Their backgrounds can be utterly different. Hans Snook was happy to drop out of university to be a credit controller at a Canadian hotel while, at around the same age, Jorma Ollila of Nokia was being selected for a scholarship at Atlantic College as one of the future leaders of the world.

The *Digerati* CEO tends to be a good listener. He doesn't suffer fools gladly and is intolerant of brown-nosers. He has his own idea of direction but tries to nudge people into a consensus to get them to buy into a common vision. As Malcolm Miller points out, being able to form and articulate a company vision is one of the key parts of the job.

The listening extends to customers. Instead of trying to force a better widget down the customer's throat, the *Digerati* CEO works with customers to find out what they want.

The *Digerati* CEO knows how to manage power but doesn't use it. He is not an enforcer but a persuader, a motivator, a pusher of people, a generator of energy and enthusiasm. He's a rare breed.

ANDREW RICKMAN

Andrew Rickman started Bookham Technology in 1989 to make optical chips then realised he lacked both technical and management skills. He enrolled in courses at two universities to do both an MBA and a PhD. He developed a new manufacturing process for optical chips, went public in 2000 and Bookham Technology immediately entered the FTSE 100 of the UK's most valuable companies.

"I didn't start out as particularly interested in electronics. I bought transistors and didn't have much success with them. I bought a kit amplifier from Sinclair, and it kept blowing up, and I wrote to Clive Sinclair and asked him for new components for it. He wrote back to me – it was either him or he had a machine which managed to forge his signature – but he wrote back to me personally when I was a teenager.

"I was brought up in an environment where all of my family were business people. My father is a lawyer, and that's a pretty independent activity, his family were all journalists, so they were fairly independent people, and the same on my mother's side. My other two brothers and sisters are all in business on their own, so the peer pressure was there to go and do something of an independent nature.

"When I was at school I started a mail order firm, and I remember borrowing £50 off a chap at school, and buying a motorbike, and about two weeks later selling it for £200. I was always looking for a way to spin a dime.

"I took jobs in my holidays in engineering companies. The internal combustion engine had a fascination for me. When I left school I got a job working in a company that built racing cars. I built one and took it home – a bit like that Johnny Cash record where he takes it home in his lunch box.

"After I left university I went abroad and worked on a sheep farm in New Zealand."

Why?

"To get away. I came back and worked for a company building racing cars. I then did the motor racing thing. That became quite an exciting activity for me. I got some sponsorship and did that on a fairly regular basis.

"I once came across a man called Damon Hill, and found myself alongside him on the grid. He wasn't a problem to beat and I beat him! That was great fun. What would be great would be if I could do that, and be a successful business person as well. Unfortunately it's very difficult to do that because you have got people who are a lot better funded than you who are concentrating purely on one or the other. After a couple of years I realised it was impossible to be a sports person and an entrepreneur in engineering.

"There are no rules in that game. You have sponsorship, and you are selling yourself the whole time, and there are all the issues involved in raising the money to do it. So it developed my skills for doing what you actually have to do to get into the car in the first place – an awareness of business, of the attitude: 'There's nothing personal about this, but this is business, and I'm going to shaft you.' "

"My philosophy is that honesty and integrity are absolutely the way to go. I've seen people successful – to a degree – in business by being blatantly dishonest. But, at the end of the day, really making it, and making a contribution, feeling good in yourself and being, ultimately, the best is the only way. It is completely down to honesty. If I trust someone, then I assume they trust me and if they break that trust then I flip completely in the opposite direction.

"After that year off, I went to Imperial College and did a degree in mechanical engineering."

Why mechanical? "Well, I think because I had been unsuccessful in making my transistor radio, and Clive Sinclair's stuff kept blowing up. I was more in tune with the mechanical side than the electronic side. If you think about it, what does electronics do for you? I'd sooner put a motorcycle gearbox together and blast down the road – you can't do that on a transistor radio.

"But I guess my interest in electronics came from the fact that, at that time, clearly the microprocessor and electronics in general was going to be a fundamental part in controlling all machinery. For instance, in the internal combustion engine you would have engine management systems and all that kind of stuff. So my real interest started when I could see the connection between my first love, and how important the electronics industry was going to be in that area. So I was very pleased when we developed a system here to measure internal pressure inside the combustion chamber.

"First I went to work for GEC, because my father suggested I should go and do something to get some credibility. And then I went to work for an American company – Genrad, a computer company.

"That got me into the computer industry. The division we worked for was in Maidenhead, but headquartered in Silicon Valley, so I'd go over there to visit and understand the culture. One thing that struck me, when I first went, was that these people weren't superhuman – they were no different to the people here – in fact they seemed to be more spaced-out than people that I had worked with here.

"What was different – it's often been repeated and its very boring to say it again now – was that nobody seemed to be particularly worried about people who made money. If you have a Rolls Royce over here, somebody would put a scratch down the side of it. In the US they'd say 'Well done.' It's summed up by Winston Churchill: 'If you want a wealthy nation, you have to have wealthy people.' "

"There was something about the environment over there that meant it wasn't a problem to do well, and that seemed to be the only distinguishing factor between the environment I was in here, and the environment over there.

"The people weren't in any way more brilliant. There isn't anything that you can put your finger on that says that people will be more innovative, or that genetically they are better, or there is something in the water. Success was just accepted. The envy element wasn't an issue. I got exposed to those cultural differences in my early twenties, and I guess that was the influence that enabled me to break out of the negative start-up culture that we had here.

"What Genrad exposed me to was the realisation: 'Here is this place called Silicon Valley. What's going on here? Blimey! People are doing really well out here! This is an incredibly innovative place.'

"There is a feeling in the UK that in the US everything is bigger and better, that money is easier to get for start-ups, that customers are easier to find, that it's a much more competitive environment, and that it's more capable. What came home to me was that it wasn't – it was purely a state of mind.

"There was a good line I heard from Hermann Hauser the other day: If you were a young chap in Europe, and you worked for Siemens, and you had a great job, with credibility, and profile, and you had your pension, and your life ahead of you, and then you gave it up to take a job at some futuristic start-up, your girl-friend would give you up. But in Silicon Valley, your girlfriend would leave you if you didn't leave Siemens to join a start-up.

So I was exposed to two different cultures – the GEC, as it then was, the 'the British can't do anything, don't take any risks' cul-ture, and the Silicon Valley culture. It was realising that people weren't different, it was simply the culture that was different and the people were just as capable – that's what set me on this direction."

His next job move was to leave Genrad for a venture capital company called Oxford Ventures Group. Why? "Peer pressure. There was no particular idea I wanted to pursue. It was just hang-ing around the pub, chatting through ideas with my mates, thinking that if you got involved in an environment where you were more likely to come across ideas and stimulation, that would be a great benefit."

He found the experience as a venture capitalist "very formative – in terms of seeing how not to do it. You could see how people were not using all the systems, and government support, and university support that was available to start a business.

"If you didn't have the initiative to go and win a Smart award from the DTI [Department of Trade and Industry], or get a BP or NatWest award, or get a bit of bench space at the local university – if you didn't have that initiative, then you didn't deserve to get any investment.

"In some respects, nobody deserves £50,000 of seed corn money, because they should be able to go out and find that money without it diluting them [i.e. without having to give away shares in return for it]. It was thinking about the model for an ideal high-tech start-up. It was not the: 'Boy, I've got this brilliant idea about how to make a widget' model, it was just the business model, i.e: 'What are the problems with high-tech start-ups?'

"You've got a triple whammy of risk:

1. Your widget – you've started developing your widget but who's to say that the widget will turn out as you hoped?
2. What happens if the market moves – and your competitors take the market away from you?
3. As a start-up you have no access to the market – you have no distribution channels – so you've got another risk there.

So the model comes about by asking how do you diversify all those risks, so that you maximise your chances of success?

"The normal Silicon Valley start-up model is: window of opportunity – technology – fit the two together – bang! My start-up model says: huge technology base – like invent a semiconductor industry basically – then start to apply it to markets."

"Another objective of the ideal model was to create something of value, where there are considerable barriers to entry. Something that takes a lot of investment and time to develop, not a flash in the pan, but a really substantial firm, and something defendable. That's an enormous intellectual challenge."

What is the purpose behind the model? "A strong desire to make a lot of money. My total measure of the business is its cash-generating capabilities, so it should be a machine which creates cash – creates value. That's what it's there for.

"The customers are not the purpose. The staff come first. By putting the staff of the company first you naturally deliver what the customers want and they, in turn, will be happy. But we don't come to work every day to keep our customers happy. We come to work every day because we want to be happy. Your customer, and making money, is the lifeblood which allows you to have fun. So it comes naturally that you would do your customer service, but I can't imagine anyone who says: 'The customer is king.' I can't believe that people will sit in an organisation, and have a miserable time, just so that customers can have a great time. Nobody would do that. Or they'd do it for about a week and then get fed up with it. We'd never have a slogan in here saying: 'The customer is king.' There's no question about it; if you've not got a happy customer you're not going to have fun. But who comes first? It's us.

"If you look at businesses that are built to last they are not driven by crude measures of business success. They have other measures. And those companies then tend to do best on the conventional measures.

"Profits, shareholder value and all those things are indicators of success, but they're not the reason people are here. Our motivation is us – making an environment which is great for us. Keeping customers satisfied, and making money are things you need to do to enjoy yourself – they're not the reason you're doing it. We're not here to make customers happy at the expense of everything else, we're here to make a happy environment for us, so we can do what we want to.

"So the business model has to reduce the risk of this triple whammy. So first of all, if you were to start off developing an enabling technology – that would be diversifying the risk, because that would be working on something which would build value for the business, but you'll be putting off having to make a decision about which version of it you're actually going to go for. So you create this generic engineering platform which means you can decide further down the line which product to actually go for. By doing that you've diversified your market risk as well, because you can now make a whole range of different things for different markets.

"The second thing is that you should develop a number of market strands and product ideas, even though you may still only be working on the enabling technology with a number of customers. So you avoid the difficulty of access to market, because you know for sure you've got the attention of someone who's going to buy, or a number of people who are going to buy, so the business model is basically a way in which you could develop a very large, substantial business."

It seems a very clinical, academic approach to entrepreneurship compared to the seat-of-the-pants, gung-ho tradition. "In analysing the success of other entrepreneurs I've often thought they didn't know why they succeeded. The issue with that is: if you don't know why it's working you don't know what to do when things go wrong."

Armed with his ideal business model, he set up Bookham Technology as a consultancy. "I soon found that the consultancy business paid me more in two-and-a-half days than I earned in five days in a job. So there were two-and-a-half days a week to spend thrashing about trying to find opportunities. I very soon focused down on the optics option in 1988."

Why? "I became aware of the advent of the optical integrated circuit or optical chip. The first thing that actually got me interested in fibre optics was a fibre-optic gyroscope. My interest in it came from my mechanical background – from knowing about mechanical gyroscopes."

The way the optical gyroscope worked fascinated him. "The principle is that you split a coherent beam of light and send it in opposite directions around a coil of fibre. If the fibre's turning, then the light will arrive back at the other end of the fibre at different times. So it's the measurement of that phase shift between the different frequencies of the light sent off. It's incredibly accurate. Fascinating – a simple principle which can measure the diameter of a hydrogen nucleus.

"That was where the awareness of optics came from. Then I thought that, in order for a device like that to work, you need integrated optics. I thought: 'Wow, fibre optics is starting to become important. Gosh, it's got an interesting application there. Wow! That sounds so exciting, so what else have optical chips been used for?'

"There's a whole load of applications; this is going to be important to a whole range of different industries. After a bit of investigation you find that research work has been going on into optical applications for telecommunications in medical diagnostics, in many different industrial applications, and there's the potential for optical computing and all this kind of stuff.

"So optics fitted the idea of finding something which had a diverse range of industrial applications. The business model was sitting ready to have optics plugged into it. It wasn't a case of producing the model because I'd found something that looked interesting, it was a case of having the model sitting there waiting for something interesting which fitted into it."

He didn't immediately see optics' potential for speeding up the Internet. In those days the Internet wasn't the overriding application for the chip industry that it is today – but he saw optics as a route to massively boosting performance in many areas where electronics was "crummy and slow". The reason why optical chips were not being used was because no one knew how to manufacture them cheaply and in volume. "The main problem was that manufacturing techniques didn't look as scalable [i.e. capable of continuing price/performance improvements] as making a silicon chip. If photonic circuits were going to be of the same scale as electronic circuits, then they had to be serving elastic markets, and therefore you've got to find a way of continually driving down their cost. You've got to find volume manufacturing techniques that are parallel to a commercial silicon chip.

"In analysing the production techniques which we researched at that time, none of them seemed to offer that. So there lies the challenge. If you could find a way of manufacturing optical circuits, in the same way that you could manufacture silicon chips, you would open up a very large and elastic market. But at that time, the knowledge base within the company was absolutely miniscule. I thought: 'Hang on a minute, let's go and get the resources we need. Let's sign up for an MBA and a PhD.' It was a combination of realising I had gaps in my knowledge, and of tapping into the necessary skills in a very economic way.

"It was all part of taking the initiative and avoiding having to look for capital. There were grants available. For instance, as a sponsored student (by Bookham Technology) I got a grant. As a company sponsoring a student, the company had to pay money to the university, but between myself and the company, we came out ahead. So my grant more than paid for the money which the university was paid. That was another modest necessary element in the overall seed corn capital."

Back in the research environment, he found that the consensus approach to making optical devices, at that time, was like the consensus in the microelectronics industry before the silicon chip was invented, i.e. if you made a transistor you made it out of the best material for transistors; if you made a resistor you made it out of the best material for resistors; if you made a capacitor you made it out of the best material for making capacitors, instead of looking, as the chip's inventor Jack Kilby did, for the optimum material for making every kind of device in one block. "People had looked at it in terms of what material would make the best device – the fastest device, the smallest device, the best performance device. This was the subject of my PhD – establishing the right structure to use.

"What was missing from a lot of research activity was an understanding of what the market required and of manufacturing technology. From a corporate research, or university research, point of view these considerations are normally left out. You leave it to other people to work out how it's going to be used, and how it might be manufactured. They might make one in the lab but it might be completely unmanufacturable in volume. That was the state of the world at that time. The big corporate laboratories seemed to have lost track of what they were supposed to be doing marketwise, and had completely disconnected themselves from the practicalities of manufacturing."

One of his high-tech heroes – Gordon Moore, who co-founded both Fairchild Semiconductor and Intel – noticed the same thing about the early European chip industry: "The lab work in Europe was always outstanding but it was completely disconnected from the engineering," observed Moore.

"It's a question of charting out the whole manufacturing path," says Rickman, "and finding out, in charting that path, whether you can prove you can do it. Because there's not much point going down there if you can prove you can't do it or, for that matter, if you can demonstrate that one way would be easier than another.

"So the problem was: How do you make optical chips on the same kind of scale as silicon chips? It wasn't that we had to use silicon but, when you analyse the various materials that were around at the time, which we did, and which we continue to do, and you do a ranking, then it turned out that silicon did come top of the list. Silicon was up above all the other materials – glass, polymers, a wacky material called lithium niobate and III-V semiconductors.

"But although silicon came out top, there was one problem – silicon didn't yield a suitable optical waveguide in the medium. Nobody had demonstrated the ability to guide light around in silicon with the right properties. It's transparent in the physical spectrum, which is a good start, and it's transparent in the near infrared which is used for optical fibre communications, but nobody had found a practical way of making the right structure in silicon with the right physical properties.

"The right physical properties are being able to guide light with very low loss, and with the same characteristics as a single-mode optical fibre guides light. No one had done that. If you unblock that problem, you win."

He unblocked the problem, but still might not have won. "When we were making the first prototypes, there wasn't enough money to do it. We were £5,000 short. I felt I was on the verge of having to go back and get a proper job, and then I won a NatWest/Sunday Times Innovation Award which was £5,000."

Another financial saviour – in a financial crunch at the end of 1991 – was the DTI. "The grant mechanisms at the DTI and within the various Research Councils are there to be used. They're not the easiest systems to tap into, they're bureaucratic and they have difficulties but they're not impossible. The people at the DTI, even when they thought we were mad, were still constructive, helpful and great. There's a strong desire to help. I think we were very fortunate."

Would he recommend that young entrepreneurs ask the DTI for grants? "Yes, because they're not dilutive [i.e. they don't involve handing over equity in the company]. If you have a very focused idea, with a very short window, you won't have time. But if you're trying to build something over a long period of time, and have got some patience, they'll be very helpful."

More funding came from the Eurpean Union (EU).
"In 1993, we started a contract with the EU to develop fibre optic components for access to the home. We led that consortium. It is

remarkable that we won that contract because all the other contract managers in the overall programme were from companies like Siemens, GEC and so on. That gave us an advance of about £160,000. For four people, £160,000 in up-front funds was better than we'd ever expected."

That wasn't the end of the EU's munificence. "At the end of the first year, we were summoned and asked to present the status of the programme. I did it, probably rather arrogantly, and most of the academic research community thought we were bonkers anyway. So I got a roasting from the European academics. Then they went off for lunch, and, when they came back, for some reason or other, their tune had completely changed and the project went ahead with doubled funding."

What had happened? "I think a lot of what we'd done, people thought was impossible. Unless they took the time to understand what we were talking about, they didn't get it. It was just fantastic. After that meeting we missed our plane, and the chap I was with and I had to check into a hotel, and I walked past his room, and the door was open, and I noticed that most of the contents of his minibar had been drunk.

"You can criticise Brussels and the EU until you're blue in the face, but if you understand the pitfalls involved, and take the time, and you don't have any choice, then it will work for you."

He takes a down-to-earth approach to the EC's largesse. "Your mission is to create wealth for the Union. And your best response is to say: 'Why the hell should I do what they say? Having got the money, circumstances might change, I'm going to go in this direction.' So being fairly bloody-minded is what's best.

"The benefits of our model are that, when you go out to raise money, if the fashion of the day is DNA sequencing, then I'm sure our optical technology can be adapted to put in a grant application in DNA sequencing." However, realising that if he was ever going to make anything, he'd need more money than could be raised through grants, he went fund-raising in 1995. One investor was Terry Matthews, co-founder of Canadian telecommunications company Mitel. He raised £1 million. The following year, he raised another £7 million from 3i and a fund set up by Robert Madge, founder of Madge Networks. "Without a critical mass of business angels you're not going to breed more successes. You need business angels because you need their expertise and the finance they can bring at the early stages, and to set an example to the next generation of entrepreneurs."

With some money raised, manufacturing could begin. Immediately he came up against a big problem. "There is a big skills shortage in the UK in terms of people who can take something out of the lab and get it into manufacturing. If we were in Silicon Valley, you would find plenty of people who have been through that process in many start-ups, but here you don't. So you have to put up with that. It's not just the entrepreneur, it's the whole management team that allows a new company to come into being and overcome all the operational issues faced by a start-up.

"We haven't got enough people who have been through the mill. It's a problem if you don't have a critical mass of expertise in taking science out of universities and putting it into manufacturing. That is something we seem to have forgotten how to do.

"We attempted to do that at the Rutherford Appleton Laboratories and the Harwell Laboratories. We cut a deal with both laboratories, rented space, utilised their infrastructure and clean-rooms. It was a cost-effective way to do it – it cost a few million and allowed us to get into pilot production. It's very difficult to operate a process unit, and control it carefully, in someone else's laboratory, but it was enough to give us further credibility.

"The manufacturing problems we solve are a sort of mechanical jigsaw. It isn't so much about where the electrons are going, it's more about putting together a jigsaw puzzle. In terms of formulating the process from the outset and making optical circuits, it was more of a miniature mechanical engineering task. We had Honeywell as an early customer. They said: 'Hang on a minute, what these guys are doing is pretty hot – it's risky – but if it's a success it's going to change the face of our business – so we've got to get involved.' Not because they believed it would necessarily change their business, but because they could see there was a risk that it would. Therefore they thought they should, in some way, be spending some time with us.

"So we were supported by the aerospace industry, by the automotive industry, and by a whole range of areas which could see the benefits of the technology. By having a technology applicable to many areas, we could find support from many sources. If you're limited to one area, then you can only get support from within that area." He is a firm believer that manufacturing has not had its day – as so many gurus are proclaiming.

"I was reading in the paper today that a McKinsey report said there would be a complete stratification of the chip industry, that manufacturing would become a cheap man's activity, and all the intellectual power would go into the design of things. Manufacturing would just become a service, and there'd be all these virtual companies. ARM is based on that virtual model. But I'd say: 'No, manufacturing's not finished.' You won't create an Intel or a Microsoft based on the ARM model. You've got to go back to something very disruptive – a change – that one day we didn't have a way of economically making optical circuits and another day we do. That's a major disruption, and a major opportunity, a much bigger opportunity to create a substantial business for industry than just cutting up an industry into layers in a more efficient way. Companies with the highest profitability are those which own both the process and the design. If you look at the ARM model, you've got a good net margin. But if you look at absolute profit from the capability that exists within that company, you're limited, in terms of revenue, in what you can achieve, because a huge value is actually being delivered by Taiwan Semiconductors (a manufacturing subcontractor) or somebody else. If you look at a company like Maxim [Maxim Integrated Products – an analogue silicon chip manufacturer] or Intel, then they have the ability to make a lot more money at the end of the day, even though their gross margin, or net margin, may not be any more impressive."

Further finance was raised in 1997 to set up a factory. Why was the finance raised in small amounts at a time? "That's the right way to do it – to reduce dilution." In other words, the aim is to give away as small an amount of the equity as possible in return for the greatest amount of capital invested. When a company is young its shares are worth little so you have to give away a large amount of shares for not much money. So the trick is to raise as little money as possible early on, so you keep as much of the equity of the company in your own hands as you can further down the line.

"If you raised all the money to solve all your problems in one go, you'd raise that money at a much greater cost to you [because of dilution of the equity] than if you raise it step by step.

"You always get wrong how much money you need. 'Enid Blyton writes the business plans of most enterprises,' according to Jon Moulton [partner in venture capitalists Alchemy, which tried to buy Rover from BMW]. He was an investor. He's a very shrewd venture capitalist. The very first venture capitalist who ever visited the company."

So raising the finance goes hand-in-hand with building the company.

"It's like climbing a hill and finding there's another hill to climb. There's satisfaction in climbing the hill – you've reduced the risk – but you've still got another hill to climb. Today, I'm standing right on top of the mountain.

"So, climb the hill, get pilot production working, the next hill is to leverage off that, get customers, get finance to build a factory, get the process running in the factory, get a new generation of products out, get more design wins, put in a better process, design wins start to create volume, production starts to take off, build new factories.

"Each hill represents the highest risk that you see ahead of you. So don't try to solve all your problems, just head for the biggest risk, solve that problem, and the value of your proposition has increased as you reduce the major risk. You now have another risk and you organise yourself and finance yourself to deal with that risk.

"I was away in Scotland last week and was phoned to be told we've just made the first XYZ chip and it worked first time. That brought tears to my eyes. I summoned up the champagne on the spot. Each hill climb is a big celebration. And by virtue of the fact that each celebration is of something that will make the company that much bigger – then each celebration is bigger than the last celebration.

"Another element of the model is chasm jumping. What's the point of following the normal business school approach to developing a company if you can prove, by jumping a chasm, it's all going to be worthwhile? A lot of what we did in the early days was running over the small hills – sort of practising if you like – showing we could do it. We knew we had to go back and do it all again. But the risks were dramatically reduced because we'd shown the path. The chief scientist is our chief chasm jumper. If you go about things in an organised structured way at the research stage, then you'll never get there – you'll run out of money.

"You've got to have people who've got massive brain capacity, who can leap these chasms, then come back and start again, and do it all properly. Those people, because of their intellect – just simple mental capacity – can trail-blaze, whereas the organised, structured person won't be able to look ahead." He's a bit of both – for instance he did well in the accounting side of his MBA. He realises there's a time for both types of activity. "You've got to know when to be focused, methodical, make sure everything adds up properly and you've got to know when to jump the chasm and cut corners. Imagine you've got two teams going forward together: in this one, you've got a brain-box; in the other one, you've got a team of methodical, organised people. The first team will win to start with, and will then need to go back to the beginning and do something else before the second team has got anything off the ground. Then the second team comes in and takes it forward."

To manage that mix of the creative and the methodical takes great skill. "What happens is that the people in top positions have to change – all the time – they have to keep taking another job. That's a big problem for a start-up. You've got to change your management team several times in the evolution towards becoming a big business. That means a lot of friction and difficulties – personnel difficulties."

How do you cope with them? "You have to get them to face up to where they're at. What they're good at. Normally people who are in a job they're not good at are stressed out. They might maintain they'd like to be there for a few months or so, but most people can't hack doing something that they find unnatural to them for more than a few months. If they realise that the role has moved on to somewhere where it doesn't utilise their strengths, then they're intelligent people and they'll move to the right role. If you can't persuade them then there's only one thing to do!

"By 1995, I had banked all this in my mind. I knew exactly what was possible. I see what we produce today as just the organisation catching up. Since 1995 I haven't seen anything different – it's just further confirmation of what was laid out at the outset. That's why, in 1995, we thought that we had sufficiently reduced the risk to bring in the big bucks. The key thing was being able to show all the functional elements of the technology. Having customers who said: 'This is good stuff.' Having all the ticks in the box to say: 'This is going to be financable.' "

With finance and manufacturing in place the team was growing and a company culture had to be established. "One of the things we said to ourselves in the early days at Bookham Technology was: 'Hang on a minute, we are starting out in a culture (i.e. the UK business climate) which is relatively negative – which lacks some of the necessary experiences and mind-sets necessary for the business to be successful.'

"At the outset of the business, people in the company had no benchmark, they had no experience about how competitors would behave. They had no understanding or frame of reference for saying: 'OK, this is how you interact with a customer, this is how you set up customers' expectations.' They hadn't got a clue how American competitors would set those expectations for customers. So one of the big issues was to develop a different business culture in an environment within the general UK environment. So how do you do that? How do you dump down here a kind of modified Silicon Valley culture?

"Probably the most significant aspect of American culture is the diversity. If you take people out of their comfort zone, and dump them down somewhere new, and you mix up a whole series of different cultural outlooks from around the world, you end up with the American business culture – and that appears to be more imaginative, and risk-taking, more determined than anywhere else.

"If you stick a management team in a room, and they are all Anglo-Saxon, they are more likely to come up with an Anglo-Saxon solution to the problem than if you have a room full of people from China, people from India – if you have some cultural diversity you will find that you have a different set of solutions. I can't consciously say that we went out to create cultural diversity within Bookham, but that's how it's turned out. Probably we're no more culturally diverse than an investment bank or somebody like that, but that's an international type of business. British engineering firms have tended not to be particularly culturally diverse. Near to where I sit are an Italian, a Greek an American, a French lady, an Australian and so forth. That goes throughout the company. I go in the kitchen and I can't understand what people are saying because they are speaking in Russian. Quite how it happened I am not entirely sure, but the benefit is that you land up with the advantage the US has – that the solutions to problems are not all generated from the same outlook on the world. And you also create an environment that breaks down the UK culture. It's like in the US where you bring everybody together from different cultural backgrounds and you end up being able to model your own culture.

"If everybody's out of their own comfort zone then you've got something you can work with. If you've got a predominant culture because of your locality and the indigenous population, then it is very difficult to change it, and it is very difficult for people from a different culture to come in and feel comfortable. If you've got a more diverse culture, then you will accept more views and you will accept people from different backgrounds."

Was this planned at all? "I could rewrite history on that particular point now. But I think it happened because when you build something from the bottom up you're very conscious of the culture and of the fact that you have really got to resist this negative culture that exists. It wasn't until I employed around five or six people that I suddenly realised that there was something different, and that seed meant that, as we grew, the business was not intimidating anybody. You could come from anywhere in the world and you wouldn't feel alienated.

"The strength of Silicon Valley is the critical mass of expertise – you click your fingers and you will find a group of people to come in and solve the problem. That lack of expertise is still a major problem over here. Two of our directors are Silicon Valley chief financial officers. We understand who we are in the race with – it's the US. We are very US-centric – everyone in senior management team is either a US citizen or has worked in the US, so we understand which race we're in. We're not in some backwater.

"What worries me, for UK industry as a whole, is the sheer pace of product development in the US – not just in this area because I think we've got it beaten – but in so many areas. It's accelerating, they are getting better and better and better at it. So it's no good us getting better when they are continuing to accelerate. It's a bit like our competitive advantage. If you are twice as far ahead of your competitors, in terms of the rate you can expand at, if you can expand twice as quickly you don't stay twice as far ahead – it's exponential – you pull away from them. And that's the issue.

"We might be starting to get it together over here but, unfortunately, even if the speed of acceleration was the same as in the US, we're still not going to catch up. So it's a worry for UK industry. We at Bookham have tuned ourselves into the US environment. One reflection of this is that Bookham is dual-listed and I think it's the only dual-listed company in the UK that has maintained, after its float, a 50/50 balance between the US and European shareholders.

"What I'm concerned about is that UK companies will look on Bookham as a benchmark on how to tune into the world's technology stockmarket – the Nasdaq – at the same time as satisfying the UK."

Why is that a worry? "Because that looks like the way to do it. You're a British company, you've got some great technology, and to maximise your financial leverage you list on the Nasdaq where they understand your technology more than in the UK. But you've got no visibility over there. You've got to work like crazy in order for people and customers and the investment community to notice you over there. You're buried in the noise which is 100 times louder than it is here. So we set an example, but behind that is years of development of the customer base and the profile of the business which has a management and board that are completely US-centric. You could write a story about Bookham, and say how we've set an example but, without saying how Americanised we have to be, it would be misleading. You can't be identified in that market as a UK company."

His final big task was to set up a management structure to run the business as it got larger. "Getting a management group able to manage a billion dollar company has been a major consumption of time and energy and we've had to change the team a number of times to get there. I'd say that was the most demanding thing – that and maintaining morale at the same time."

How do you do that? "The only way was to get people to follow. I had worked out the equation – the model – but to get other people round to my way of thinking would take too much time. You could articulate some of it but no intelligent person would spend the same time as I could in the analysis. So inevitably they had to have a degree of faith. So to get people fired up I just had to get them to follow."

Why would they follow? "Because I've got a vision, motivation, a set of values that they shared; I inspired them and made them believe we would deliver the elements they needed to fulfil their own objectives and desires."

Eventually came the moment, familiar to all entrepreneurs, when he realised he didn't have to do it all himself – that the momentum was self-sustaining.

"Two or three years ago, I woke up one day and realised this thing had gone super-critical. I didn't need to be in on every decision to drive the technology in the direction I believed it would continue to go – in the direction I had set. I had anticipated that change would happen at some moment in the future. I realised that the moment had come by testing. I would say: 'This is the direction I want to go in,' and I would leave them to get on with it for a few weeks. Then I'd check a few data points, and see that my vision had got diluted, and they were losing it, then I'd put it back on the rails and say, 'This is the way we're going, guys.' "

"The transition to hands-off came at the point where the direction of the company was stable but the problems were far bigger than I could load into my brain – and I needed lots of people to solve those problems – and if the vision in that group was going in the right direction then they should be allowed to get on without being interrupted. About a year after that came a switch round to understanding that the technology was no longer my intellectual challenge. No longer could I come up with the world-beating elements of our technology – I was now too distant from that, I had done my piece, and had inspired a whole group of people who would be far more capable at it than I would ever be, and my time was wasted doodling on the back of an envelope trying to come up with good ideas for technology.

"Then it became entirely a matter of leadership and inspiring people within the company and outside. It also became a matter of developing a senior management team. The leadership is now a leadership team, it's not just down to me. We're now moving into a phase where the organisational model is the main challenge."

Did he have any role models? "David Simpson has been my mentor, he has a phenomenal range of experience, and I gained insights from Robert Madge and Terry Matthews who both invested in Bookham. Jack Kilby, the co-inventor of the electronic chip with Robert Noyce, is on the board of Bookham and has been very helpful.

"In a rather arrogant way, I'd say the first seven years of Bookham was like the Fairchild period of Robert Noyce and Gordon Moore.

"I'd say the challenge that faced us was greater than faced them. The reason for that was because they were in an environment that allowed them to develop their technology to a particular level. The direction it had to go in was clear and they created a company out of something that was already proving itself to be commercially viable. What I did was to go back a step before that. The new challenge was to be the boffin who might not know where his invention would go – to pull the technology, kicking and screaming, out of the laboratory, and then to build it up to reach something that approximated to what Noyce and Moore had when they left Fairchild Semiconductor to found Intel. So here was I, in a big corporation, developing an idea and one day realising it was very significant, and realising that the corporation was doing it rather badly, and I could take it off somewhere else."

That's very much the typical scenario for a Silicon Valley start-up.

"Bookham was not like that. Bookham was like going right back to the inventive stage, and starting down there, and pulling together a body of knowledge in this area, and rounding it up, putting it in the right direction and getting it to the Fairchild stage, and then taking it forward. That, to me, is more challenging and more difficult than Fairchild's challenge. But I'm not there yet in terms of what Robert Noyce and Gordon Moore did. Bookham still has a distance to travel to be to optical networking what Intel has been to the PC industry. Every sign is that we will get there. But we're not there yet."

His ambition – to achieve success on the same scale as Noyce and Moore – is breathtaking. Robert Noyce and Gordon Moore founded the two most successful companies in the history of the chip industry – Fairchild Semiconductor and Intel – and Intel is one of the world's ten most valuable industrial companies. But he makes no apology for his ambition, pointing out that you have to aim high to enthuse your backers, your employees and your customers.

"My understanding is that Noyce and Moore were not aggressive individuals – they don't appear that way – but they built a team and a culture which delivered a ferocious approach to business."

What is he concentrating on now? "On boosting links with universities. We take a lot of undergraduates in summer holidays and students in their sandwich years."

His favourite business book is: *Built to Last* [3rd edn, James Collins and Jerry Porras, Random House Business Books, 2000].

The greatest joy in his life is, "Getting married, having children."
He's cheered seeing a better outlook for venture capitalists and
entrepreneurs. "Yesterday I went to VentureFest – a major venture
capital start-up conference. I was the guest speaker yesterday and
Hermann Hauser is the guest speaker today. I was driving down
the road and there was a sign – *a sign!* – taking me off the A40
to this event. I have never been to a venture capital fair or conference on the scale of this conference before in the UK and I
thought, Wow! This is really brilliant, this is absolutely fantastic! I
had almost marginalised this type of event because I have been
so depressed by them in the past when you roll up and there's
the same old audience – badly attended and miserable. But here
was something incredibly positive, a real reflection of the fact that
times are changing."

What's the biggest mistake he's made? He seems surprised by
the question. "I'm an optimist so, if I ever made a mistake, I'd be
looking to turn it to my advantage. If reality clicks in that the team
is going to under-perform, you can't say it's all over, because
everyone would go home. So you have to flip into the mode of:
'Well, this is where we're at, we're not at the top of that hill, we're
at the top of this hill, and we've got to get over to that hill, so how
are we going to do it?' We've made some progress, we've learned
some lessons. It's a bit like research, you go down avenues, you
find one's wrong, so you go down another avenue. You've learnt
something, so it's not a waste of time. You publish your results
and say: 'This doesn't work, don't do it.' "

Has he had any catastrophes? "No. Bookham has never had a
catastrophic cock-up. Many start-ups have catastrophic cock-ups
and survive them but I think those businesses which avoid them

are the more successful ones. If you have a really terminal problem – you run out of money, the board blows up, the CEO gets fired – then you tend to lose good people, and others will catch up on you."

What are his special skills? "The ability to take the company through its various stages and balance the technology, the manufacturing, the people, the customers and the financial environment. Getting the best team and motivating them. I can sense just from a glance across the room whether somebody is firing on all cylinders or whether there's a problem. In the early days, if I asked someone how they were getting on and their eyes whizzed around in their head I'd just know, 'That guy's just been for a job interview with our competitors.' You can tell."

What gives him the greatest feeling of success? "There are 850 people here all doing something that stems from my idea and my leadership – that's a tremendous success."

What effect has it had on his family life? "This is very much a joint thing for my wife and me. We have our life plan with our children, I do one bit of it, and she does the other bit – we've divided the work up and off we go. You can't do what I've done without having a family life that's built on very, very solid rock. You can't do something like this without creating a platform of security for them – a bedrock – which is why you should make sure you have the downside protection. Like, when I was doing the PhD and MBA I had the downside protection of knowing I was investing in myself as a marketable entity.

"My downside protection was: 'I'm in telecoms, I'm in communications, I've got a flipping PhD and I've got an MBA and I had a decent job before I started all that. So I could probably get a decent job afterwards.' One difference between here and the US is that people always say: 'Aren't you worried about the risk?' "

What is the best way to raise finance for a start-up? "Only finance to the next milestone otherwise you'll be diluted out of sight. Never take any investment in your company other than in common stock – never take preference shares – you want everyone, shareholders and staff, to be aligned to the same agenda and if they have different classes of stock they have different agendas. One of the most important lessons I've learned is to make sure everyone's interests are aligned – for instance make sure your backers' interests and your needs are aligned with the same agenda, or you might find they want to liquidate their shareholding at a possibly damaging time."

What would he say to Tony Blair or Gordon Brown?

"Look, you say you're supporting enterprise culture but, in the period of this government, the taxation on enterprise has got worse. So the enterprise environment – which is primarily driven by the taxation environment – has got worse.

"That's down to the government's inability to implement its plans. I'm very positive about the policies of both the government and the opposition. Everybody's got the message that we ought to have an enterprise culture. But unfortunately the whole mechanism – the Treasury, the Inland Revenue, the civil service – is not able to work efficiently enough to put it in place. It's not down to political intentions, it's down to the ability to execute. The debate should not be about what's wanted but how the government should implement its plans. "So I'd say to them: 'Stop talking about politics and start running the country. Start making the civil service do what you want it to do.' "

Like many high-tech entrepreneurs he's vexed by the stock option situation. "Stock options are taxed on the basis of the capital gain between the grant price and the exercise price. The Inland Revenue taxes them like PAYE at the time they're exercised. So you pay a huge tax bill when all you've done is pay out money – you haven't actually got anything."

He sees an anomaly in Europe: "Everything's getting worse. Europe's getting less competitive in terms of employment legislation, tax, red tape. It's all becoming more difficult for enterprise, just as the social environment and the general consensus are moving more positively and the enterprise culture is coming through.

"But I don't think in terms of national boundaries any more. If this environment doesn't provide your operation with what you want, you just move it somewhere that does. So why moan? In technology you're serving a global market so you've got to go to the place with the best environment. The other point is you can get upset by obstacles and culture but the thing to do is craft a new culture which you build to avoid as many of these problems as possible."

The Bookham Odyssey has not moved entirely as he would have wished: "It's taken longer than expected because of technological problems. The problems we've solved are just mind-boggling. It's a very, very tough industry. You can be eternally optimistic but you still have to outperform other people and others are employing ten times the resources we have on these problems – though we're still ahead of them."

When will he be satisfied? "I won't be a happy man until Bookham is a $50 billion company, turning over billions of dollars each year, and being highly profitable. We've created

something of considerable value here which will have a
phenomenal impact in our industry, but I'm not finished. I'm not
satisfied yet."

Why does he do it? "It's not a get-rich-quick approach, it's a
built-for-life approach. It's not to get to a lifestyle position –
though that comes with it – but it's the satisfaction of the entrepreneurial spirit, and the intellectual satisfaction of creating this
thing of enormous value – not the money side of it alone but the
overall impact of it. You can't be motivated to do something like
this for money alone; it would never, ever keep you going."

GORDON MOORE

G ordon Moore founded the two most important chip companies in the history of the electronics industry – Fairchild and Intel. Both became the world's No. 1 chip company and Fairchild invented the chip industry's production technology, while Intel was the first company to commercialise memory chips, and also invented the microprocessor. He is also famous for 'Moore's Law'. Intel is one of the ten most valuable companies in America and, in 2000, *Forbes* named him America'a eleventh rich-est man. He is Chairman Emeritus of Intel.

Moore was born in a small town on the Californian coast where his father was deputy sheriff and his mother's family ran a shop. He says it's the only town in California to have remained the same size for sixty years because the main road bypassed it.

When Moore was ten, his next door neighbours gave their son a chemistry set for Christmas. Playing with it together, the two boys developed a fascination for causing explosions. It not only set Moore on the track to becoming one of the greatest chemists of his generation, it also taught him that chemistry was something which produced tangible results – you could do things with it.

Doing things with chemistry was to occupy Moore for the next sixty years and, almost incidentally, made him the richest man in California with a fortune of over $10 billion. He is a great man in the sense that he has always pursued great objectives and achieved them handsomely. As he wound down his working career he pursued new directions in helping both scientific research projects and environmental conservation programmes around the world with his time, advice and money. He's also a great man in a personal sense. An interviewer notes that you could spend a week with Moore without ever finding out who he is. He'd never tell you. He fits the Anglo-Saxon heroic mould – understated, unassuming, disdaining to speak for effect – the thoughtful person to whom people turn at times of uncertainty.

When you meet him, you have to make all the running. He answers any question with great consideration, deliberation and candour, but is disinclined to lead a conversation.

He was educated at Sequoia High School, San Jose State (where he met his wife, Betty), the University of California at Berkeley, and finally Caltech where he was awarded his PhD in 1954. His first job was as a university researcher, but he was soon spotted by one of the most renowned scientists of the day – the co-inventor of the transistor, William Shockley.

In 1955 Shockley had set out to make money by commercial-ising his invention. With backing from the instrument manufacturer Arnold Beckman, he set up a company in Palo Alto, California. The following year he was looking around for talented chemists and was told about Moore. Moore – no doubt influenced by the lessons of his neighbour's chemistry set – thought doing something which would end up in a product would be more interesting than research for the sake of research, and Shockley wanted to make a truly revolutionary product – a silicon transistor – which promised to be the main building block for all future electronics systems.

So, in 1956, Moore joined Shockley Semiconductor. He was 27. He started on a Monday; the Friday before, another new recruit had joined – Robert Noyce – with whom Moore was to co-found both Fairchild and Intel.

However, shortly after he'd joined the crew, the Good Ship Shockley changed tack and sprung several leaks. Shockley decided to drop research into the silicon transistor and instead develop a four layer diode. A four layer diode was a laboratory curiosity rather than a revolutionary new product which would change electronics manufacturing.

Cracks were also appearing in the company infrastructure. 'Shockley was an amazing man", recalls Moore, "good on problems, not so good with people. His physical intuition was unsurpassed. One colleague said: 'Shockley could see electrons.' But he had a peculiar idea of how people worked. He asked someone once what would make his job more interesting and the guy said he'd like to publish some papers. Next day Shockley came in with a paper and said to the guy: 'Here, flesh that out and publish it.' "

Shockley's odd personality led to some curious events. "We had a clerk who ripped her hand on a door," remembers Moore. "Shockley was convinced it was malicious and was going to put the entire staff through a polygraph test. He was paranoid. Once he fired a guy he thought would steal secrets. The guy was a Cuban who found out that Shockley was an insomniac and kept ringing him up in the night to keep him awake."

The company's address – 391 San Antonio – was rechristened by staff 391 Paranoid Place. Others noted Shockley's difficulties with the simplest features of daily life. David Packard, founder of Hewlett Packard, was amazed when, one day, Shockley asked him where to buy pencils. Moore was disappointed that in his time with Shockley, "We never developed a product, or even defined one."

Moore and others went off several times to see Arnold Beckman to try to get him to sideline Shockley but, though initially sympathetic, Beckman felt that the award to Shockley of the 1956 Nobel Prize for physics for the invention of the transistor made it difficult to displace him. Eventually, Shockley's eccentricities provoked one of the seminal events in the history of the semiconductor industry. In 1957 Moore, accompanied by six colleagues – Jean Hoerni, Eugene Kleiner, Jay Last, Sheldon Roberts, Vic Grinich and Julius Blank – walked out on Shockley. Later on, Robert Noyce also left to join them when they realised they needed a leader.

"The idea of setting up a company never occurred to us. None of us had an entrepreneurial inclination. We thought we liked working together and decided it would be nice to find someplace to work together. We hoped that a company might hire the entire group."

"Someone [Eugene Kleiner, later to found the famous venture capital firm Kleiner, Perkins Caufield and Byers] had a relation in an investment brokers who knew Arthur Rock, a Harvard MBA. He said: 'Why not set up your own company?' We sat down with the *Wall Street Journal* and went down the names to see who might want to set up a semiconductor company. We asked 30 and got 30 No's.

"By coincidence we ran into Sherman Fairchild. He came out and talked to us and decided to invest $1.3 million, in starting up a company. No one in the founding group of Fairchild had any management experience. The first thing the eight of us did was to go out and hire our own boss. We interviewed a few people and appointed a guy called Ed Baldwin. Baldwin came from Hughes."

Sherman Fairchild's company was called Fairchild Camera and Instrument. Headquartered on Long Island, it made military cameras. It made the cameras that detected the build-up of missile sites on Cuba preceding the Cuban Missile Crisis of 1960.

"Sherman Fairchild required all his people to go through a psychology test. Noyce and I read each other's results. They said we were good technically but we would never be managers."

Fairchild Semiconductor was established in California to pursue the development and manufacturing of silicon transistors. But soon came a much bigger prize – the invention of the chip itself – essentially a collection of transistors and other components on the same piece of material.

Fairchild shared the patent on the chip, or integrated circuit (IC), with Jack Kilby of Texas Instruments. However, having invented it, the Fairchild founders seemed a little unsure of what to do with it. "After we introduced the first IC, we thought: 'We've done ICs, what shall we do next?' "

The world was not particularly impressed. "The first ICs were not received enthusiastically by customers. Systems designers did not like being told that their function was going to be incorporated on the chip. The breakthrough came when Noyce said: 'We'll sell the ICs for less than they can buy the individual components.' "

In 1959, two years after starting the company, the parent, Fairchild Camera and Instrument, exercised its right to buy out the shareholdings of the eight founders. Each got $250,000. In its third year, Fairchild was one of the world's top ten semiconductor companies. In 1965 it was No. 3, behind Texas Instruments and Motorola, and went on to be No. 1.

"The exciting thing about Fairchild was that everything was a surprise. That we made these things, and people bought them, was a surprise. Fairchild had this mine of technology – it was ridiculously rich. We had more ideas than we could exploit; one of them was planar technology."

The planar process made possible the manufacturing of chips. To this day it is the fundamental process technology of the chip industry.

Fairchild devised the photographic (photolithography) method of manufacturing chips using ultra-violet light which is still used today, and invented the batch process – by which a number of chips are made together on one silicon disc which is then sawn up into separate chips. The batch process is still the means by which all commercial chips are made.

Noyce and Moore also established a management style suitable for their unusually intellectual workforce. The goal was egalitarianism. Corporate hierarchy was out. There were no visible signs of rank, no corporate limos, no reserved places in the car park ("If you were that important you got in early"), no individual offices (everyone had the same sized cubicle), no dress code, and anyone could challenge anyone else if they thought they had a better idea. The purchasing policy was that anyone could buy anything they wanted so long as no one else objected. It was a company culture in which each individual was expected to take responsibility for their decisions and to internalise the common values and goals. The values were engineering values. "We tried to let the best technical brains make the technical decisions."

The culture became the model for Silicon Valley companies and has since pervaded almost every industry in almost every developed country. But it was an alien notion in the 1950s, causing continual friction with Fairchild's East Coast parent with its traditional buttoned-up, top-down, dirigiste corporate style.

Just as significant for the future of the semiconductor industry as the technology and the culture they developed was Fairchild's role in pioneering the Silicon Valley spin-off model.

It didn't take long for the Fairchild model to be copied. "A few years after we started Fairchild," remembers Moore, "Ed Baldwin took a few people, and the process, and set up his own company. That was the first spin-off."

The company Baldwin set up was called Rheem Semiconductor. "The Rheem spin-off really bothered us. Frankly we felt a sense of betrayal and when we found that they had all our process specs we were doubly discouraged. With subsequent spin-offs our attitude depended on how people behaved when they left, but a lot of the stuff wasn't that protectable. We hated to see good guys leave. The group that put the first IC into production went off to start Signetics [later sold to Philips] and General Microelectronics took one of our best guys and told him: 'Here's an empty building, get us into the MOS [Metal Oxide Semiconductor] business.' "

In 1965, Moore made the most quoted prophecy in the industry's history. "*Electronics* magazine wanted a prediction for their 35th anniversary – it turned out to be amazingly accurate." Moore looked at the pace of integration being achieved in the Fairchild laboratories and concluded that the number of components that could be put on a chip were doubling every year. Ten years later, he revised that to every two years. Although 'Moore's Law' is often quoted as being 'every eighteen months', Moore asserts: "I never said that."

It is not only the most quoted prophecy in the electronics industry, but a rule of thumb which every electronics company assumes when it is making plans based on the technology's capabilities over the next few years. It has also been the target which chip companies set themselves. So Moore's Law has been more than a prophecy – it has set the course of the most stupendous increases in price/performance ever seen in any industry at any time.

Many years later, asked when he first noted the trend behind Moore's Law, he replied with his typically simple honesty, "When I was writing the article."

After ten years of unparalleled technical and commercial success, Fairchild ran into management problems. "The situation was getting complicated, the chairman was really a bit of a buffoon – nobody paid much attention to him. The board of directors fired him and then hired and fired another one. The logical candidate was Bob Noyce, but they wouldn't give him the job. I had the best job in the industry running the Fairchild lab but the situation didn't look stable in the long term. Bob decided to leave and I decided to leave with him and see what we could come up with."

Following the departure of Noyce and Moore, Fairchild progressively lost its way. "That's when Fairchild hired Hogan [Lester C. Hogan, president of Motorola Semiconductor] and an army with him. It was an unusual way for people to join a company. The whole thing that was Fairchild was destroyed in that period. Hogan's army took all the top jobs. They didn't know the company at all."

There followed a period of decline at Fairchild which ended with it being bought by the French oilfield services company

Schlumberger, which lost over $1bn trying to turn the company round.

"Schlumberger was a victim of hubris. They'd been successful with everything they'd touched but they got Fairchild at a time of deterioration. I'd far rather start a company from scratch than try and fix a sick one."

Eventually Fairchild was sold to National Semiconductor which, in the mid 1990s, sold it to a consortium of financial institutions to raise cash to pursue its (failed) attempt to make clones of Intel's microprocessors. So the Fairchild name was resurrected and the company survives as a stand-alone entity again.

According to the *Palo Alto Times* of 2 August 1968, leaving Fairchild meant, for Noyce and Moore, a chance to "get back into the laboratory."

"The timing was quite good. The idea of semiconductor memory was around, and we reckoned we needed to make a 200:1 cost reduction to be in competition with core memories" (magnetic cores were used for memory storage before chips came along).

"It was also a time when it was very easy to raise money. We called Art Rock and we got calls from people wanting to put money in." Later Rock said that raising the money took as long as it took to make the phone calls – a tribute to the reputation which Moore and Noyce had built for themselves. Noyce and Moore each put in $245,000, and Rock himself put in $10,000. All but two of the eight founders of Fairchild invested money in the new venture. Over the next two years Intel raised another $2.16 million in private share placements and went public, raising $6.8 million in 1971. Thirty years later Moore's six per cent stake was worth $10 billion.

"Intel was a tremendous opportunity for us to have it all go round a second time. It wasn't such a surprise to us as it had been when we started Fairchild. This time things happened much as we expected them to happen. We didn't have the problem of how to get management experience of big companies because Fairchild had become a $150 million company with 20,000 employees, so we had the experience."

Leaving Fairchild with Moore was his assistant director of R&D, Andy Grove. A refugee from the 1956 Hungarian revolution, crushed by the Russians, Grove (christened Andras Graf) had learnt English while working his way through New York State University and had gone on to take a PhD at the University of California at Berkeley. "Andy Grove we hired right out of school," recalls Moore.

After considering a raft of names – e.g. Calcomp (California Computer) and Elcom (Electronic Computer) they settled on the name Intel (Integrated Electronics). The company was extremely quick to set up its first factory and had a product out in 1969 – a bipolar RAM. "It didn't cost so much in those days. We developed two technologies (Schottky bipolar and silicon gate MOS) and put our first three products into production for $3 million. We made the right bet on both technologies. Bipolar was too easy – others could copy it – but silicon gate MOS had the right degree of difficulty. It was seven years before we had competition – that gave us a chance to expand in a vacuum. The opportunity we had to get established was the result of the fortunate choice of silicon gate MOS technology."

In a blistering period of innovation and expansion between 1969 and 1971, Intel was the first company to make and market a

DRAM, a SRAM, an EPROM and a microprocessor. "The DRAM and SRAM were obvious," says Moore, "but what kind of surprised us was the microprocessor. The idea of the company was to make complex pieces of silicon and sell them widely. We aimed to get design costs down and amortise them over a long production run. But the microprocessor's potential far exceeded anything we could have imagined."

The reason for that potential lies in the then unique characteristic which microprocessors brought to chips – programmability. Until the microprocessor came along, if you needed a sophisticated chip you had to have one specially made, which was expensive. However, the nature of chip manufacturing – with its high fixed costs – meant that the most economical way of making chips was to have long production runs of the same kind of chip.

When the microprocessor was invented, Moore succinctly summed up its significance: "Now we can make a single chip and sell it for several thousand applications."

The contribution of the microprocessor was that it allowed the smaller original equipment manufacturers (OEMs) to buy a chip off the shelf and program it themselves to do whatever they wanted it to do. Because it was off the shelf, it came relatively inexpensively and, because of the effect of Moore's Law, the microprocessor, and therefore the products it went into, got continually more powerful and capable. Accordingly, the microprocessor both reduced the cost of manufacturing electronics products and opened up the industry to many more companies and entrepreneurs.

That was particularly the case with computers. "The microprocessor democratised the computer," says Ted Hoff, who invented it. The microprocessor made the PC industry possible and made computers sufficiently affordable to be in every home and on every desk.

Hoff was Intel's 12th employee. He remembers getting a phone call in the summer of 1968 from Noyce, who was setting up the new company, then called Noyce Moore Electronics but soon renamed Intel. Noyce was looking for R&D people, and a professor at Stanford had recommended Hoff, who was an assistant professor at the university.

"I was interviewed before Intel had a building," recalls Hoff. "I went to Bob Noyce's home for the interview. I had been talking to people in the semiconductor industry about what it would take to make semiconductor memory. Noyce asked me what I thought was the next area which semiconductor technology should explore." Their minds were on the same track.

The company was incorporated in July 1968 and Hoff joined in September. "The day I joined was the same day Intel moved into its first building – 365 Middlefield Road, Mountain View." He remembers Intel as: "a very exciting place to be. We started off developing two new processes – Schottky bipolar and silicon gate MOS. Developing a process is a horrendous task. It's like walking on the edge of a cliff – if you're not close enough to the edge you're not competitive; if you're too close you fall off."

He recalls the feel of it. "There was a tremendous spirit – a sense of doing the impossible. Noyce wandered around chatting to everyone. In this kind of business you need to encourage a degree of creativity – you can't chain people to a bench and get them to crank out the numbers. Sometimes ideas come at the oddest times – the result of interactions between people – two people are discussing a problem and one of them asks the right question."

"There was a key invention at Intel at the same time as the microprocessor," Hoff recalls. "The fellow at the next bench to me – Dov Frohman – invented the EPROM. It seemed like the ideal thing for program development. So I built an interface that allowed the microprocessor to read a program out of EPROM. We made that available to customers – essentially it was the first design aid."

"There was a tremendous amount of focus from management," continues Hoff. "The fact that they'd had the Fairchild experience meant that they saw the problems that come from success. They saw the effects of inattention to detail and they set out to make sure they didn't make the same mistakes – they did a beautiful job. Each of them had different philosophies but they worked so well together. Like the way the succession was handled. At first, Bob Noyce was at the head. He could break free of past traditions and do something new – he was the most adventurous of the three. As the company became more established and growing, Gordon took over. He was more conventional than Bob but more futuristic. Then, when the whole company could have got out of control, Andy took over. He's hard-nosed – keeps everyone on target. The loss of Bob Noyce [he died of a heart attack in June 1990] was a great tragedy. He was so charming, so sharp, you never had to explain anything to him twice."

So hard-nosed was Grove that he instituted a late list for latecomers to work. Typically Moore assumed this applied just as much to him as to anyone else and remembers running in from the car park to get there before signing-on time.

Even when Intel was one of the world's ten most valuable companies, and Moore was its chairman, he still didn't have his own parking space, once complaining: 'We have so many people in Santa Clara [Intel's HQ] that if you leave during the day, it's difficult to get a parking space when you come back." There can't be many people in his position with the same problem.

Others remember the early Intel days with similar feelings of excitement to Hoff's. "If you wanted to do wonderful things, Intel was the place to be," says Federico Faggin, who put Hoff's idea of the microprocessor into a working design on silicon. He joined Intel in 1970.

One of the early disasters was Intel's 1970s diversification into the digital watch business which was then a high-profit activity, but this soon changed. Intel bought a digital watch company called Microma in 1972 and sold it in 1978. Moore still wears a Microma watch.

"That's my $15 million watch. That's what it cost Intel to get in and out of the watch business. The gold plating's mostly come off now. By the time Intel came out of the watch business, the chip cost less than the push buttons on the side of the watch."

The broad progress of the company was steeply upwards, however, and it hit the $1 billion annual revenue mark in 1983. It may have looked like an inevitable progress from the outside, but Moore doesn't remember it that way. "I wonder what would have happened if IBM had chosen Motorola's processor instead of ours – this industry is based on tenuous factors."

While Intel rose to become an industry giant, the Silicon Valley effect of new companies spinning off from old continued. Naturally Intel was not immune. Had the spin-offs bothered him?

"Seeq was the one that bothered us as much emotionally as any of them did," Moore replies. "We lost momentum. So long as people do it on a reasonable basis we can stand it. If they take trade secrets, we'll try and discourage them; if they go off with the knowledge in their heads – we can argue about that. But everyone's got the right to do it."

Gordon Campbell, who led the Seeq spin-off in 1983, recalls receiving a writ from Intel at his home in the middle of the night. He was one of the ones to be 'discouraged'.

Two years later, it was quite another matter that was troubling Intel. The Japanese had hit the market the previous year with vast quantities of higher quality memory chips. Intel was losing fistfuls of money.

"In 1985/6, the world semiconductor industry lost $6 billion – the US lost $2 billion and Japan lost $4 billion – all the US memory producers dropped out; none of the Japanese producers dropped out."

Andy Grove recalls asking Moore what a new boss of Intel, coming in from outside, would do with the memory business. "Get out immediately," was Moore's response.

Intel did so. The cloud had a silver – or rather golden – lining, because it meant that Intel concentrated its efforts and resources on microprocessors. It also decided to end its licencing policy for microprocessors.

In 1988 the *New York Times* wrote: "The personal computer industry and Wall Street are just waking up to the fact that Intel has one of the most lucrative monopolies in America."

The newpsaper could not have been more right. From then on Intel's revenues and margins sky-rocketed. Ten years later, Intel was one of the world's ten most valuable companies. Moore's personal shareholding of 6 per cent – valued at $15 billion by *Forbes* in 2000 – made him America's eleventh richest man.

Of the two companies he has founded, which does Moore regard as being the most important? "Fairchild may have had a more dramatic impact than Intel," he replies. "Fairchild developed the planar technology which was a significant difference to what was done before. Most of the early MOS work was done there – Fairchild has most of the patents on CMOS."

Had he been surprised by anything in the way in which the technology developed? "Not really," he replies. "I'm surprised how dominant MOS has become over bipolar – now 90 per cent of the industry is MOS. It's a discouraging thing, this convergence of technology," he grins. "Back in the 1960s the Japanese didn't know what to do, they were trying to track the technology and it was zigging and zagging. The worst thing we did was to make it predictable – now everyone is making the same CMOS structures. I'm also surprised how robust the technology has become without us coming across any limits. Density has gone up ten thousand times. The business has been phenomenally elastic – the number of transistors produced doubles every year."

Although credited as the industry's wise man, he plays down his ability to foresee future directions.

"In the 1960s I turned down the idea of semiconductor memories as something that didn't make much sense. In the 1970s someone came to me with an idea for what was basically the PC." He always says he turned it down because no one could come up with a better use for it than for storing recipes.

Although he was the leading technologist of his generation, he's no blind technophile, and suffers the same frustrations with the products of technology as everyone else. "I absolutely do not want a phone in my car; if someone wants to call me they can get me some other place. The telephone on my desk has all kinds of buttons and functions – I've no idea what they're used for." He says he was "the only Intel executive that travelled without a laptop computer. I tried it for a while but it was such a hassle going into a hotel and making a connection – I was ready to throw it out." Talking about his house, he says, "It's not like Bill Gates' house – if I want to change a picture I have to take one down and hang up another one." [Gates' house has flat-screen displays on the walls so the pictures can be changed electronically.] "I thought we'd have a few microprocessors in the house but my wife Betty said we'd got to have plain switches."

As someone who has been intimately involved in the twists and turns of the chip industry from its beginnings, he has a philosopher's detachment from the worry of continually working on the edge of success and failure. "It's a peculiar business. The only sane strategy is to bet the company regularly. A conservative position – trying to live with the existing generation of technology – is a strategy to put you out of business fairly rapidly. You have to keep investing in the next generation of products and technology – you'll never get well on the old products – it's always the next generation that drives recoveries in the business cycle. I'm not sure that we do still bet the whole company any more – we're probably not betting the company's total existence – we have a pretty big base now – but our position in the industry depends on our ability to drive the technology – we hear footsteps behind us all the time."

Like many successful Americans, he uses part of his wealth to fund new companies, so helping to perpetuate the Silicon Valley effect of new companies spinning off from old.

"I participate through the VC (Venture Capital) funds – to do it individually takes too much time – I get the funds' reports; they're part of my general education, I guess."

He's a great enthusiast for the Silicon Valley model – a model which he did more than almost anyone else to invent. "If there's anything Europe lacks it's this entrepreneurial activity we have in Silicon Valley. Start-up companies are marvellous for bringing new technologies to the market. Big groups develop the technology in the labs and small groups take it to market." One of the things he thinks is good about the Valley is that: "It's OK to fail – we've all done it. In Silicon Valley there's no stigma to failure. That's an important part of this area. New companies set up with no regard to risk." He holds to the belief that: "If you're not failing, you're not trying hard enough to do new things."

Moore is well-known as a life-long fisherman. "I'll fish for anything – trout, marlin, anything." It was the fact that some of his fishing haunts were being affected by pollution which helped motivate his current involvement in conservation.

As well as using his wealth to support start-up companies, he uses it to contribute to scientific purposes and to his conservation efforts. He gave $35 million to Conservation International – a group of scientists who collect and share information on how to preserve biodiversity. Among others have been a $15 million donation to materials research at the University of California at Berkeley and $1.3 million to Oregon Graduate Institute. In 2000 he gave £7.5 million to Cambridge University in the UK to set up a science and technology library. "The University of Cambridge has a long history of doing leading research into some of the most fundamental questions that mankind can ask," he said. "I find this exciting and uplifting and am pleased to contribute where I can." In November 2000, he announced his intention to donate $5 billion to a foundation he is setting up to support high-end educational intitiatives.

He says he's not a planner – letting his diary get filled by others who want time with him. Apart from fishing, he likes, he says: "Computer games which don't take more than a few minutes – like Minesweeper or card games."

He retains the engineer's down-to-earth assessment of technology's capabilities and limits. Asked about often-repeated predictions that computers will one day take over from people, he replies in his measured tones: "If we can't figure out how to keep ahead of computers we deserve to get taken over by them."

He has described himself as a revolutionary and, in the sense that the technology he is responsible for developing is disruptive, he is right. It overturned the computer industry. It put the high technology industry in the hands of engineers rather than Big Business. It created a business model that has spread to every industry and to every industrialised country. But you wouldn't expect him to claim any of that. The most you can get out of him is: "I think we played a pretty central role in what's going on in information technology."

SIR CLIVE SINCLAIR

To the general public, Sir Clive is the best known figure in the UK electronics industry. To the electronics industry he is a pioneer whose company once sold more computers in the US than any other computer manufacturer. He trail-blazed for many of the UK's successful high-tech entrepreneurs and for today's 'Cambridge Phenomenon'.

Almost from infancy, he knew what he wanted to be. "There was an inventor on a radio programme called Toytown who invented a radio, and a paint that changed colour, and all sorts of things like that. I was six or seven at the time."

What was attractive about it? "It just sounded exciting. It sounded an exciting thing to do." He was hooked.

It could have been in the genes. Both his father and grandfather were engineers. His grandfather was a naval engineer who designed battleships. As significant, in view of Clive's commercial career, was that his father was also a salesman. The son was to show a natural talent for salesmanship when the time came. But in the early days life was all about inventions. "I was always interested in inventing. First it was mechanical calculators. Then I got interested in electronics." In 1958, at school – St George's College, Weybridge – he designed a one transistor medium wave radio and started writing articles on electronics for magazines, one of which was *Practical Wireless*.

In common with the later breed of techies personified by Bill Gates, he found formal education tiresome. "I got fed up with school and didn't want to go university. I was educated up to A-level standard and, after that, I educated myself. When I left school at 17, I became a technical journalist on *Practical Wireless*. The company which published *Practical Wireless* also published *Practical TV* and *Practical Mechanics* – it was a series which had been started by F.J. Camm and I worked in the next office to him. I was hired as editorial assistant. There was an editor, an assistant editor, and me. Shortly after I joined, the editor fell ill, and couldn't come back to work, so the assistant editor, who was 27 or so, was made editor. He was afraid of F.J. Camm who was a bit of a daunting character – though he never bothered me – and he had a nervous breakdown. So I ended up running the magazine on my own – which was fairly easy, it was only a monthly. I did it for a few months and then became an editor at a tiny publishing company called Babani's which still exists. So I ran that for three years and then Mr Babani of Babani's offered me the job of running Bernard's Publications – at a hugely greater salary.

He was without any formal electronics training or education, yet he was writing and editing books and articles which were principally about electronics. Recognising that he needed academic knowledge in order to do the job, he set out to teach himself electronics.

"I was very good at maths and physics at school, and I was able to teach myself very rapidly. I found I could teach myself much faster than I could be taught. Because I was interested in it, learning was very easy."

He wrote many books, mainly about the use of transistors as receivers and amplifiers. Although invented in 1947, the transistor was still regarded by many engineers designing electronic products in the early 1960s as a new-fangled device, and many preferred to use the tried and tested glass vacuum valve. Hobbyists, excited by the new technology's promise, were keen to know as much as possible about them, and were avid readers of magazine articles and books explaining how to use them.

"I didn't have to write the books myself, but it was quicker and more fun than finding authors to write them. They were for hobbyists – nothing terribly sophisticated."

In 1962, he moved from Babani's and became technical editor on a professional electronics magazine called *Instrument Practice.* Later that year he established his first company – Sinclair Radionics.

"I wanted to be an inventor and the only way I thought I could do that was under my own steam – which I am sure was right."

Ask him if there was anything in his publishing career on which he looks back with particular pride and you get a very firm reply: "I don't look back. Not at all. I'm interested in the future, not the past."

The initial offer of financial backing for his company fell through, and the fledgling company had to find a way to generate income. "I looked around for opportunities." One came in the area he knew best – transistors.

"I did this deal – the first deal I ever did – with Plessey Semiconductors who made transistors under licence from Philco in the US and sold them to the computer industry at very high prices. I bought the rejects."

Financing for the deal was somewhat unorthodox: "I managed to borrow half the money from a girl I knew. Although they were rejects, they were very good transistors – they simply hadn't met the various specs put on them. For those days they had very high frequency in comparison to anything else – 15MHz – which was dramatic in those days. They hadn't made the specs required by the computer industry but, for the purposes which I was selling them for – which was audio and RF [radio frequency] devices – they were absolutely perfect, beautiful."

As he says this, a wide smile comes over Clive's face: "They were so nice." He may claim he doesn't look back, but there are some things which obviously don't fade in his memory, and one of them is a nice transistor. "I tested them, and gave them four different brand numbers for different gain categories, and wrote a book on how to use them – published by Babani – and did articles in magazines about them. I also put in ads. I sold those transistors very well."

That could be another reason for his fond memories of them. 'I bought them for a shilling (5p) each." he says. The advertisements he ran at the time to sell them quote prices ranging from seven shillings and ninepence (38p) to fifteen shillings (75p). Enviable margins!

The cash flow of the business was also enviable because, while buyers sent money with their orders, Clive could get his advertisements published on credit. "There were three magazines, really, in those days: *Radio Constructor*, *Practical Wireless* and *Wireless World*, so I advertised in those. Fortunately they didn't bother to check up on me because, when I placed the first ad in *Radio Constructor* I didn't have any money. I was going to pay the magazine with the money I got from the orders. Which I did. I just assumed that people would send me money and that I would have the money to pay for the ads. And that's what happened. The cash flow was great."

He explains the enthusiasm for the transistors. "In those days there weren't many options on where to get transistors." Transistor-making as a commercial activity started after 1952 when AT&T, owner of the transistor's inventors, Bell Labs, licenced companies to manufacture them. By 1962, there were still relatively few companies – and they were mostly American – who could manufacture transistors. Those companies wanted to sell to big professional users, so hobbyists and low volume buyers could find it difficult and expensive to get their hands on them.

"That was the start of the business really. I don't know how much money I made from the transistors. That was the first deal, then I went on buying them and bought loads more."

The financial viability of Sinclair Radionics was established by the transistor deals, but they weren't fulfilling his ambitions. "My whole intention had been to make products – to come up with innovations. I designed a tiny amplifier which was the first product, and I sold that in kit form." The kit included some of the ASM transistors, and cost 28 shillings and sixpence (£1.42). "The smallest of its type in the world," claimed the ad. It was three quarters of an inch long by half an inch wide. "Simple to build using ordinary tools," said the ads. Were there problems with people not being able to assemble them?

"Loads, as ever," he replies. "We had people servicing them. The kits sold very well. And then I did the first little radio." Called the *Slimline,* it cost 49 shillings and sixpence (£2.45) which evolved into the *Micro-6* and then the *Micromatic*. "I did a lot of radios. I don't know how many I sold but it was lots." In 1963 he appeared on the front cover of *Practical Wireless* with a radio he'd designed especially for the magazine billed as 'The smallest radio in the world.'

The following year, Sinclair Radionics expanded into the hi-fi market with amplifiers, tuners, stereo decoders, loudspeakers and power supplies. The hi-fi market was expanding rapidly on the back of the transformation from valves to transistors.

For the next three years, Sinclair Radionics grew rapidly. In 1967, its turnover topped £100,000 and the company moved to Cambridge. The decision was almost accidental but it had important effects. "In 1967, I had a little office in Islington, and a friend of mine had a company in Cambridge – Cambridge Consultants – and he had a chap who was working for him to do the mail order for me. He left the company and we rented some space in a village outside Cambridge. Then it expanded more and so I rented a house in Cambridge, and I moved there, and we had the business established there for quite a few years. And then I went to the Mill, in Cambridge, eventually."

The move had far-reaching effects for the UK electronics industry because many of the brightest and most successful high-tech companies followed Sinclair's example and started up in Cambridge. Today it's one of the world's most dense conglomerations of high-tech businesses – known as the 'Cambridge Phenomenon'. Was there a plan? "It was just a question of invention. A question of: 'Where is the world going? Where do the opportunities lie?' All the time I was keeping tabs on what was happening. From very early on, long before we were in

Newmarket Road (the Cambridge offices), I started working on electronics watches – long before they existed. And then we were first in the pocket calculator business because we discovered this method of getting the power consumption down."

The problem with making a pocket calculator was the greed for electricity of the display. This was before today's LCDs (liquid crystal displays). In those days LEDs (light emitting diodes), which emit light and require a lot of power, had to be used. Power is the enemy of portable products because battery life has to be adequate if they are to be attractive. Sinclair's innovation, which made the pocket calculator possible, was a pulsing power supply, rather than a constant power supply, which reduced the amount of electricity needed. That meant smaller batteries were required which made possible a slimline, pocketable product. The result – the *Sinclair Executive* – was nearly the first pocket calculator in the world. Hewlett-Packard beat it, by some three months, with its Model 35 launched in July 1972. The *Executive* cost £79 – a revolutionary price for those days.

It was one of Clive Sinclair's most satisfying lifetime achievements. "Because what we did there was to make an extremely slim one – ours was only nine millimetres thick and everybody else was making great clunky things, much bigger than ours, we managed to reduce the power consumption by a factor of between ten and thirty times because we could switch the chip on and off without it losing its data, so it was only on for very brief periods. So we got the power consumption right down, so we could run it off these little tiny button cells. Nothing like that existed in the world and it sold very well in the US as well as over here."

A tribute to Sinclair's design is that the company which made the chip for the calculator, Texas Instruments, used the same chip in a pocket calculator of its own which was larger and more expensive than the *Executive*. Another accolade to the pioneering *Executive* is that it is now on display at New York's Museum of Modern Art. As well as winning many design awards, the *Executive* earned £2.5 million in export revenues. The next model – the *Cambridge* – did even better, becoming the UK's top-selling calculator. In kit form it cost £29.95. Fully built it cost £43.95.

"Then we did the world's first single chip scientific calculator – the first cheap one too [it cost under £30]. We did that by taking an existing Texas Instruments chip – which was a four function [add, subtract, multiply, divide] chip. Texas Instruments had made it internally programmable – you could change the ROM – but it had only three registers. We reprogrammed that, much to their amazement, to create a full scientific calculator. A friend of mine, Nigel Searle, a computer scientist, did the programming, and I did the algorithms because no algorithms existed at that time which would have worked in just three registers. We went to Texas, stayed in a hotel room, and did the whole job in a few days. We took the programme in to them, and then went back and collected the chip. Texas Instruments were completely baffled by this. There was a chap at London University, a professor who specialised in algorithms, and he couldn't figure out how it could ever be done in just three registers. He thought it was technically impossible."

At this point another broad smile spreads across Clive's face at the recollection. He radiates pleasure. 'Exciting times," he says.

Also ephemeral times. No one rests on their laurels for long in the high-tech industry. "The calculator business boomed. We did terribly well, but then the world competed. Eventually we got driven out of it because we didn't have control over the key components. The Japanese did, particularly the liquid crystal displays (LCDs), and we got to a position where we simply couldn't compete. So that was the end of that."

But not quite. Bad luck breeds bad luck. "Gillette approached us and wanted to make calculators under licence. We designed one for them. But Gillette were completely hopeless. They hadn't got a clue. They made a complete mess of the business. Every time I try licencing people it turns out that way."

Suddenly he remembers something: "Actually, I hope it doesn't, because I'm just about to do it again!"

It was time to move on. "We had started developing electronic watches many years before they first appeared. We would have been way ahead of the field because we had the chip for the watch working long before anyone else, but then the people processing the chip – Philips – gave up that process. It was absolutely devastating.

"So we went to STC who said they'd set up a similar process from scratch – just for us – which they did. And we put the watch on the market."

The famous *Black Watch,* launched in 1975, had a black display and you pushed a button to read the time displayed on a red light-emitting diode (LED). Sold as a kit, it cost £14.95. It caught the imagination because nothing quite like it had ever been seen before. Even the advertisements were pioneering, including one of the earliest uses of the new meaning of the word 'cool' as in: 'Styled in the cool, prestige Sinclair fashion.'

However, they also said: 'Easily built by anyone in an evening's straightforward assembly' and 'From opening the kit to wearing the watch is a couple of hours' work.' That was not the experience of many purchasers. The difficulties of putting the *Black Watch* together, and getting it to work, led to its commercial failure. But so stylish did it look, and so unconventional was its design, that the Swiss Horological Society exhibited the *Black Watch* at their Royal Horological Fair. By then Sinclair Radionics was feeling the pinch. It had heavy R&D overheads, but no calculator business, and a failing watch business. The company went into loss and sought financial support from the NEB (National Enterprise Board) which had been set up by Harold Wilson's Labour government to support companies in strategically important industries. The NEB didn't impress Clive. "Complete and utter idiots. I got fed up with them and left the business.

"I left and started Sinclair Research. That was the start of the computer business. That shot up. My idea was that if you could make a computer cheaply enough, then people would buy it just to learn about computers out of interest.

"At that time the cheapest computers were £700 or so, and that was worth a lot more then than it is today. We brought one out at £100. We did that by some innovations which nobody noticed at the time because, years and years later, people started to do the same thing thinking it was something new."

What he did was to double up the tasks which each chip had to perform. "In those days you had the central processor and you had memory for that, and then you had video memory and a video processor. I scrapped all that and just had one processor – a Z80 – and one block of memory – and it did everything, it drove the display directly and it ran the keyboard.

"There was terrific cost advantage in that, because there was no special video processor and video memory and we also had this very small RAM – 2K in the first machine – so you could choose whether to use more display space in the RAM or more programming space – it was a very efficient use of RAM. The letter keys doubled up as control keys, with control functions on them, and it really turned out very nicely indeed."

Sinclair's first computer product had been a kit, called the MK14, which was first sold in 1978. The MK14 had a National Semiconductor microprocessor, 256 bytes of RAM and its sales were managed by Chris Curry – later to co-found Acorn Computers. Then came the first fully-built computer and the one which made the company's fortunes, the ZX80. The ZX80 was launched in February 1980. It was the first computer in the world to cost under £100. It measured 9 × 7 × 2 inches and weighed 12 ounces. It boasted 1Kb of RAM. The fully-built price was £99.95 and it was also offered as a kit at £79.95. The ZX80 was an instant hit. Over 100,000 were sold in the 18 months it was in production, 60 per cent overseas. More successful was the ZX80's successor, the ZX81. Launched in March 1981, it was marketed in the US as the first computer ever to be sold for under $100. In the UK the price was £69.95. In its first two years in production the ZX81 sold over a million units.

"In the ZX81, which used off-the-shelf chips, we got it all down to four chips which was dramatic really because hardly anyone else had anything less than 70 chips in their computer. In fact the lowest at the time was 44 chips."

The ZX80 and ZX81 have a place in computer history. Like the Apple II in the US, they made computers something which ordinary people felt they could buy. In fact they made ordinary people feel they were obliged to buy them. As word got around that the computer revolution meant that children would be disadvantaged if they couldn't use computers, parents sent off for Sinclair's computers in droves. The success helped Sinclair's suppliers. For instance, Psion, then in its earliest days, wrote the flight simulator for the ZX range and found itself selling all over the world on the back of the ZX's success.

This success also bred many UK rivals. Oric Computers, Dragon Computers and Acorn Computers were just three of many. Acorn, founded by Dr Hermann Hauser and Clive's ex-sales manager, Chris Curry, had a great success when the BBC set up a programme based on the Acorn range to teach people how to use microcomputers. Later the microprocessor designed for the Acorn was spun off into a separate company – ARM Holdings – which is now quoted on the FTSE 100.

Sinclair was about to enter a rollercoaster ride of fabulous success followed by disaster. In 1982, Sinclair Research launched its most successful commercial product – the Spectrum. It had colour, 16K of RAM, cost £125 and sold five million. A 48K version cost £175. It was fabulous. It led to Sinclair Research being, briefly, the biggest seller of computers in the US. Sinclair Research boomed, a placing of shares through the City raised £14 million for Clive and the Queen gave him a knighthood.

But disaster beckoned. It came in four blows. First there was the Timex debacle. "We did a licence agreement with Timex and again the problem was that they thought they knew better than us what the product should be, and when we brought out a new model of the Spectrum they delayed for over a year. It was a complete waste of time and we lost our market lead."

Then there was the technical triumph, but commercial failure, of the flat screen TV: "We had been working on it long before we did the computers." Development cost Sinclair Research £4 million. "The flat cathode ray tube was the only one ever done, anywhere in the world. It was the only one which ever worked. It was a lovely thing. A lovely little tube, and we designed and built a factory to make it. We did everything ourselves, and we did this chip for it which would be remarkable even now, and really unbelievable for its time. It was one chip and it had all the TV on it except for the tuner and a few high-voltage transistors at the output. It was automatic multistandard – it worked automatically on NTSC, European PAL or English PAL – so you could take it anywhere and it worked.

"I had tried to get into pocket TV back in the 1960s because I missed the pocket radio market, which had been terrific, and I thought it would be fantastic to do the same thing with TV. In 1966 I nearly came out with a pocket TV – not a flat screen TV, but a pocket TV – using a lot of those ASM transistors. We didn't get it onto the market because we didn't have the money. So it took years and years to get pocket TVs onto the market and, when they did get onto the market, it didn't turn out to be as big a business as expected.

"I can rationalise that now because people want to look at a big screen, but we didn't know that at the time, and I'm still surprised there was not more of a market. Of course people still make pocket TVs now, but they don't sell in great quantities. It could be that people don't like to look at something so small – that it's a strain on eyes to watch something so small. We lost quite a lot of money on that."

The third disaster was the QL. This was to be a small business computer – the first SOHO (Small Office Home Office) machine. It was launched in January 1984 with a price tag of £399. Instead of the Zilog Z80 microprocessor which the ZX range used, the QL used the much more powerful Motorola 68000 microprocessor. Disaster hit when the company ran into manufacturing problems and the promised 28 day delivery time on the QL was extended to six to seven months.

The fourth disaster was a horrendous mismatch of supply to demand in the computer industry over Christmas 1984. "The computer business had been a huge financial success and then everyone got into it and inevitably the market collapsed and we had a very big problem with overstocking.

"The problem was that every year the shops had ordered more for the Christmas market. Then one year they found they had over-ordered, and they threw them all back at us. So we had a big cash flow problem that year, and the end result of that was that we sold the computer side of the business to Amstrad.

"We did that deal over Easter 1985 because we had cash problems. Alan Sugar was on holiday in Florida, and he was doing the deal on the phone. We had all the creditors at a meeting in London in the solicitor's office in the City. There were dozens of them. They were so intent on getting the deal sorted out they worked all through Easter – literally three nights in a row. I couldn't believe that the lawyers could go without sleep for such a time. I couldn't believe I could have done it either. But we did. And the deal was stitched up. I remember the outline of it being written down, and it was all deadly secret, and the paper blew out of the window and fluttered down Fleet Street.

"And so the deal was done. Originally Alan Sugar wanted to buy Sinclair Research – the whole company – but it was decided it was too complicated to do it in a hurry, so he bought all the computer range and the use of the name. And that was fine. He was a very nice guy to do business with."

After the wild successes of the Spectrum, the flood of wealth and the apparently unfettered opportunity to pursue whatever paths of invention he wanted, wasn't this a tragic outcome?

"I didn't see it as tragic. It was sad because a lot of people were thrown out of work – but they did well – a lot of them started businesses as a result. But I never look back. It's sad if you dwell on these things, but I never do. I always believe in looking forward to the next thing. I get on with it. Of course it was a sad event but I don't see it as tragic – more as a lot of lost opportunities, and a waste of a lot of resources."

The lost opportunities lay in the research work. "When the company was very rich, we were able to pursue a lot of research avenues such as waferscale technology and parallel processing computers."

Wafer scale integration is a way of combining microprocessors with memory on one chip to make parallel processing computers. "I had a long-term idea of making highly parallel computers which I thought was the right way to go, and still do. PCs ought to be parallel machines. They'd be many times more powerful if they were. I'm sure it will happen eventually. It could have happened ten years ago. Our route to making a parallel processing PC was through waferscale integration via Anamartic which was spun out of Sinclair Research."

He still has a hankering to make a parallel PC, and would if he could. But it's too expensive a venture. "If I made a lot of money I'd have a go at it. It's something I'd like to see happen. Something I'd like to be part of."

Despite his current interest in electric vehicles, computers remain close to his heart. "I have been thinking about doing another computer for a long time, because I so despise the current PC architecture and design. It's such a complete and utter technical mess, it's appalling. I remember seeing the first IBM PC when it came out. I had a look inside that and I thought 'My God, how can they get away with that?' It was such an awful design, and it hasn't got any better. These things are absolutely antediluvian – a dreadful piece of technology with horribly complex, over-engineered chips using vast amounts of power – when there's a beautiful ARM chip there that could be used."

For the moment, it's not computers but electric vehicles which are taking up most of his thinking. "I've always thought electric vehicles were a good idea. When new legislation allowed anyone over 14 to drive one, we decided to do the C5.

"I still think it was a good idea, but it was probably wrong because it was too low down. But we sold a lot of them. I would like to do the same sort of thing again. I'm sure that sort of product will happen."

Nonetheless he regards the C5 saga as his biggest mistake – not because it was done, but because of the way it was done. "Doing the C5 on such a large scale was a mistake. It was done that way to get economies of scale. We should have done it on a smaller scale, which would have reduced the cost and we'd have learnt from the process.

"Even the best ideas can fail in the market place. When we showed the C5 to people, they liked it. But we got a very bad press. The trouble with the press is that it's a distorting mirror – it exaggerates. To the press a thing is either great or it's a disaster. It says that what you're doing is fantastic, when it's really not, and vice versa. The press wants a story, so they go one way or the other. The press is merciless. I've been friendly with journalists, but I don't go out of my way to make friends with them."

He's obviously thought a bit about why he got a bad press on the C5: "People fear change. That's quite right – change frightens animals – it's natural. So it was wrong to come out with a radical product and throw it at the public.

"If you're just making an existing, familiar product which is cheaper than existing products – that's OK. But the C5 was something radical, and that causes resistance. It should have been brought out slowly – like Mercedes did with the A-Class which is a great success."

After the C5, Sinclair Research continued with electric vehicle drives in the form of power packs to assist bicyclists, called Zeta. The concept has been expanded to wheelchairs. He's also been developing ultra lightweight bicycles. "Bicycles weigh 22 lb. What I've tried to do is make a bicycle which weighs a quarter of that, and is very compact, and you carry it around with you –

on the bus or wherever. It's very difficult to do because bicycles all use the same basic parts so they all weigh the same. The crank, axles, etc. all use heavy metals so, to make a lightweight bicycle, you have to re-design every part of it. We did this and went through a first generation product, and the Scottish Highlands and Islands Development Board were going to back it, but then a new managing director came in and dropped the project."

It was one of many frustrations he has experienced as original thinking comes up against the stolid wall of conventional thinking. "I always thought pocket calculators would be a good thing and indeed they were. It was hard to imagine that people wouldn't think so. But when I was bringing them out, I tried to get people like W. H. Smith interested in them, and I couldn't – they couldn't see the market. It was very frustrating."

To Clive, it feels wrong that a product which could be invented, isn't. "It's astonishing how we fail to exploit things. Many things are not adopted or even explored. For instance, Hull University developed a process for drawing polyethylene and weaving it which, when heated, became as strong as steel but nine times lighter. But it's not been used. It's baffling that these things don't get taken up – just as it's baffling that parallel computers haven't happened.

"What makes things happen? No one knows. I used to think inventions would come when technology permitted them. But they don't. The bicycle didn't come along until the late 19th century – but it could have been a century earlier. And the car didn't come along until the end of the last century – about a century after the technology became available. Cars are such an attractive thing. It's strange they weren't invented much earlier. The Wright brothers themselves couldn't understand why flight hadn't happened fifty years before. That's interesting, because it means there are things we could be doing now but we're not – like parallel computers, for example.

"Something that we could do now, but I expect won't happen soon – if at all – is personal flying cars. All the technology is there to make personal flying machines. There are a lot of technologies coming together now to make it possible: GPS (global positioning systems) for navigation, small but powerful computers to control them and cellular phone systems to guide them, because I don't think you'd want people flying them. They'd have to be automatic vehicles.

"The problem of vertical take-off has meant you need a very high power-to-weight ratio engine which, in the past, meant you needed gas turbines which are very expensive. However, now you could use electric motors which have just as good a power-to-weight ratio and are cheap.

"You could make nice vertical take-off flying machines. You'd use fans for vertical take-off and wings for forward flight driven by fuel cells. Tilt rotors would be a very nice way to do it, or tilt wing, because they could do three or four hundred knots without any trouble."

Maybe because he doesn't dwell on the past, he's not reflective when it comes to examining his life. Ask him if he's learnt anything from his successes and he says: "I'm not sure I did. I don't know really. Nothing in particular."

But he's learnt something about himself. "I know I'm not a good runner of businesses. I find it very stressful. I did it badly and didn't really like it. So I've adapted my methods to avoid running businesses." Friends like Nigel Searle and Michael Pye have allowed him to avoid the business side. "Success is not a one man band – it has to happen in a group."

Ask him what he's learnt from his failures and he says: "That it's very difficult to know in advance what's going to be good, and what's not going to be so good."

Asked if his business life turned out as he intended, he replies: "Oh no. I didn't intend Sinclair Research to go from a huge business to a small business."

Of all the many products he's come up with, the one which gave him the greatest satisfaction was the scientific calculator, probably because he did something there which was entirely cerebral and which astounded conventional industry and academic thinking. Much of his motivation lies in the pleasure of astonishing people. "I'm trying to change the world a little tiny bit. I'm trying to introduce an improvement, so that people will say 'Goodness, that's nice'."

He's not a political animal. What would he say if he had thirty seconds to make a pitch to Tony Blair? "I don't want thirty seconds to pitch to Tony Blair," comes the reply. The most important of life's lessons he'd pass on is: "The Kipling thing – 'To meet with triumph and disaster and treat those two impostors both the same'."

But he's more forthcoming to would-be inventors: "You need to be a pluralist – to have knowledge on a lot of fronts but, if necessary, to be able to go deeply into a subject. To be able to learn, and go on learning, and to believe in one's own ideas."

Does he have any advice for others? "I'm short of good advice."

That's strange for someone who showed a generation that it was possible to become a worldwide player in computers and consumer electronics from a UK base without any real capital. The genealogy of much that happened later in the UK electronics industry sprang from Clive – Psion started off by writing software for Sinclair products, Clive's colleague Chris Curry left to found Acorn Computers with Hermann Hauser using Clive's business model, and from Acorn sprang ARM and a host of other Cambridge-based companies such as Virata, Cambridge Silicon Radio and Element 14. Acorn's technology went to form the basis for Pace Microelectronics. Amstrad took over Sinclair Computers and consumer products and took them on to much bigger things. Andrew Rickman of Bookham was first exposed to electronics when buying a Sinclair kit as a boy and was enthused when Clive personally replied to him about a problem.

In high-tech businesses there is always a family tree behind success. Innovation and ideas are passed around a community and spawn new ideas and new companies. That's how Silicon Valley grew – and still grows – and it is how Cambridge is growing now. The person who started all that off by having the effrontery to challenge the American computer industry, and show that it could be beaten, is the man whom an entire generation came to know as 'Uncle Clive'.

DAVID POTTER

Born in South Africa, David won a scholarship to Trinity College, Cambridge and was awarded his doctorate by Imperial College, London. He lectured in the USA and UK, while successfully investing on the stock market, then set up Psion to participate in the microelectronics revolution. Twenty years later, Psion entered the FTSE 100.

David Potter's self-confidence was nurtured early by his mother and grandmother who brought him up in Cape Town after his father died prematurely. Nowadays he points out that half the CEOs in the FTSE 100 lost their fathers at an early age – speculating that it spawns self-reliance, which breeds self-confidence.

Childhood triggered three motivations: pleasure in the life of the intellect, the thrill of building things and the satisfaction of making a buck. His grandfather, a professor, stimulated the love of ideas; a desire for exotic toys made him build things like go-karts; and commercial success as a teenaged photographer developed his taste for business.

In his early teens he struggled over whether to become an academic or a builder of things, deciding: "Academics comment on what they see; builders make things happen."

At 18 he won a scholarship to Trinity College, Cambridge. The family was living in Zimbabwe during the country's independence struggles which made family finances difficult. He had sold sandwiches to support himself as a student and continued the practice at Trinity, selling encyclopaedias to American servicemen and ice creams to tourists in Hyde Park. His unusually loud voice helped when gangsters muscled in on his patch in the park and he loudly warned them off. To this day he cites the incident as something which boosted his self-confidence. Another was physics – the "Queen of Sciences" he calls it. "Physics deals with the simplest things," he says, "but develops an inquiring mind and a methodology for understanding and analysing any kind of problem: academic or practical; inside or outside physics. Physics gives you a humility about ideas and theories – the fact that the nine out of ten of them are wrong, conditions you in the business sense. Physics teaches you to always test ideas against a mathematically demanding framework which is not true in, say, economics. The lesson of physics is vital in other fields if you're to impose rigour, and a cold, hard attitude to ideas. I love ideas, the trouble is that mostly they are wrong. The important thing is to identify those which are true, or real, or have great value – and that's terribly true in business."

Cambridge exposed him to a brighter, broader, peer group which stimulated his competitiveness. The 1960s revolutionised British life. He revelled in *Beyond The Fringe* and the satirical movement. The legacy of his South African/Jewish mix was a tolerant, pragmatic, intellectual mind-set, uncomfortable with established thinking and happy in the iconoclastic university culture. He worked hard, loved the life, got his degree and won a scholarship to Imperial College. He recalls a "wonderful double life" of intellectual and social activity in London. He was using computers for the first time to work on non-linear physics to model and simulate many kinds of complex physical behaviour.

In 1968 and 1969 he went to the USA for summer work and to lecture, and published a book, *Computational Physics.* He became a full-time lecturer working a lot in the US but, unlike other academics, his teenage interest in business had made him an avid watcher of the economic and business scene. Although he found the rigour of economics more limited than physics, he found the subject matter interesting. From the other side of the Atlantic, the UK in 1974, seemed to him "crazy" with Prime Minister Ted Heath's three-day week, the miners' strike and the stock market crash. He invested his savings in the stock market – in Racal and GEC among other companies. By 1975, the market had begun to recover and he'd doubled his money.

He came back to the UK and invested in smaller companies which he had thoroughly analysed. The exercise both taught him about business dynamics and made him £100,000. Half of it he invested in a house – at his wife's insistence – and the other half was the seed capital for Psion. It was time for the builder to take over from the intellectual. His inspiration was the invention in the 1970s of the microprocessor. "It was obviously going to have the most profound impact on the world, and here was my opportunity to participate in a phenomenon of great importance." The teacher in him searches for an analogy: "Say you were a painter – think what it would have been like to have been an Impressionist, in 1870, in Paris."

"There's a time and a place, and you're part of a great movement. You're sharing with lots of people a community which has set about changing the world. That's the way I saw it.

I could see this was going to be profound, and I wanted to participate in it."

His business instincts appreciated the opportunity. "It's difficult to enter businesses where there are established, ossified markets but, when you get certain kinds of economic change – or technological change – then great new opportunities open up and the little guys are at an advantage because they're more innovative, they're less structured – so there are huge opportunities. That's why I founded Psion."

He resigned his lectureship in June 1980. In August he bought an off-the-shelf company and named it Psi. "Psi stood for Potter Scientific Investments – or maybe it was Instruments – one or the other. I abbreviated that to – the Greek letter psi – and I thought, that's a funny name, a nice name, it's terrific! Then I did a trade search and found there was a company in California called Pacific Steamship Inc. so I couldn't have that name. So I threw in the O N because I thought of Exxon which is a very large company, and we've got to be ambitious. And I thought that having O N at the end sounded high-tech like neutron, proton, electron etc. When people ask me what it stands for, I joke: 'Potter Scientific Investments Or Nothing' – it's partly true, but not 100 per cent."

Next, he had to find a way for Psion to make money. The first microcomputers were beginning to appear. "I thought that I would look at the software on these things to see whether I could find a gap or opportunity. I knew there would be gaps and opportunities – it was just a question of identifying them."

He went into research mode. "I read computer magazines, and found out what people were doing, and wrote letters to them, and sometimes would call them and say: 'I'm Dr David Potter – I can play the PhD game just like they can – I got my foot in the door all over the place. I'm good at networking, and making contacts, and so I researched it. Then I began to see some little opportunities which I tested in the market empirically – initially by publishing software – which meant I didn't have to spend a great deal of money employing expensive development people."

At the time, the microcomputer (precursor to the PC) was just emerging. In America, the Altair and the first Apple microcomputers had appeared on the market.

"In this country there was something called CPU in Cambridge which was Hermann Hauser and Chris Curry and there was Sinclair Research which came up with the Z80 microcomputer in 1980. Then I saw what Hermann Hauser was doing – he produced something called the Acorn Atom – and I began to examine how they were selling them. I rang them up and said: 'I need to come and see you'. So I went and chatted to Clive Sinclair and Hermann Hauser. What I was doing was searching for opportunities."

He then looked at the software being produced for these microcomputers and found "a whole cottage industry going on". One example was a British Airways employee who'd written a chess program to run on a Z80. "He was advertising in funny, dirty little Xeroxed magazines saying 'If you've got this kind of computer – a Z80-based machine – and if you put in a few bits here, and a few bytes there, you can play chess on your machine'. Wow! It was really interesting stuff.

"So I approached some of these people and said: 'If I make a deal with you – a non-exclusive deal so you can carry on selling your stuff yourself – and I repackage your product and sell it, I think I can get it distributed much more widely than you realise. And I will give you a 12 per cent royalty."

So Psion kicked off as a software publisher with a whole range of products, from the cottage industry developers of computer games to utility products such as printer drivers and databases. With his relationships in South Africa, he helped Acorn and Sinclair set up distributors over there and also participated financially. That gave him the entree to markets across the whole of Europe because Sinclair and Acorn began to develop their business model all round the world and Psion could use these distributorships to get into a much wider market. "My publishing activities began to take off. In the first year, turnover was £120,000 and I made £12,000 profit after paying my salary. The thing was rolling, and I could see that I was going to make a great deal more the following year."

He was so confident because experience of publishing software products showed him how to develop them. "I thought I could outdo all these people. I wanted to make products which would interest people and show them what can be done on these strange computer things. I wanted people to say 'Wow! That's an amazing thing to do'."

In May 1981 he invited Charles Davies, who had read for his doctorate under him at Imperial College, to join Psion. "He was the first person to join. By then I had turnover and profit and I was satisfied I wasn't gambling with Charles' career because he is an earnest person."

Charles nearly did himself out of a fortune. He was offered ten per cent of the company but only two weeks holiday. Feeling aggrieved, Charles took the agreement to a solicitor who advised him that, because Psion was a small and risky enterprise, it was better to have the bird-in-the-hand of an extra week's holiday than the bird-in-the-bush of some dodgy shares. Less than twenty years later, the shares were worth £60 million.

Together they pondered on what they could produce that had the Wow! factor. The answer was a flight simulator. "It was done with the ZX81 which had all of 32K RAM which had to be loaded off a tape and you played it on a television. Then we produced it for the Sinclair Spectrum and we sold millions, we made a fortune out of that. It was brilliant.

"Because we were highly skilled, we knew the aerodynamics, and we actually used the real equations of aeroplanes, and we worked out the way to treat the view from the cockpit. We asked ourselves: 'When you're sitting in the cockpit, what do you actually see?' and: 'How are going to simulate that on screen?'

"We worked out the equations for transforming that three-dimensional geographic world onto a two-dimensional screen showing runways, lakes, trees, mountains and everything. It was actually a beautiful bit of work. We had great fun. We worked out some of the theory together, and Charles implemented it in the computer. We produced a great product and sold millions."

Although Psion's proprietary products proliferated, the publishing side continued and the head-count grew.

"We had an East End/West Indian character working with us – a very bright fellow – his mother was a Cockney and his father was West Indian, and he had this extreme Cockney accent. We had this game with this funny little character like Pacman with an endearing look to him and we didn't know what to call him, and this guy came in with his Cockney accent and said, 'Why don't you call him 'Ungry 'Orace?' So we did – but with Hs – and we did a whole series with Horace. Horace went on to do anything – he went skiing – and there was Horace and the spiders – he had to battle against these things. These are the origins, the genesis, of the games which people play now, and we were part of creating that. It was great fun." But it was not all fun and games – spreadsheets and databases were added, called VuCalc and VuFile.

In Psion's second year of trading, the turnover was £1.6 million with a £600,000 profit achieved on a capital base of a few tens of thousands of pounds. "It was a very nice return on capital – 10,000 per cent."

The following year, turnover was £3.2 million and profits were £1.6 million. Return on sales was 50 per cent.

"We were the best. We led. I forged relationships with Sinclair where they were selling everything under their label – Sinclair – but marketed as 'from Psion'. I supplied them in volume, at low prices, and we were still making 70 to 80 per cent gross margin and so everywhere the computers went, so went our products. It was, dare I say it, a monopoly."

The way Psion started, first researching the market, then distributing other peoples' products for a royalty was a low capital entry into the electronics market. Instead of the proverbial garage, Psion started in some rooms at the back of an estate agent in Maida Vale, rented for £40 a month. The first piece of office equipment was an electric typewriter with a duff '*m*', bought for £150.

"As we began to sell more and more of this stuff the stock began to float out onto the corridor and into the estate agent's offices so he kicked us out. That's when we acquired Huntsworth

Mews, which was 3,500 square feet, which we've still got." It's still used by an associated design company.

By the summer of 1982, Psion employed 30 people, and cash was pouring in. The microcomputer market was taking off, and Psion – on the back of major deals with Acorn and Sinclair – was being swept along. An approach from the notorious publisher Robert Maxwell was rejected. Maxwell later created 'MirrorSoft' – software programs distributed by the *Daily Mirror*. "I actually knew all about the Maxwells because my wife was a journalist, and I used to go and fetch her on Friday evenings at the *Sunday Times* offices. So I knew all her mates socially, and I remember having a furious argument with one of them in the Blue Lion opposite the *Sunday Times* offices, where they used to hang out, and he gave me the goods on the DTI report on Robert Maxwell."

Success had its worries. "At the end of 1982, I said to Charles: 'We're making giant amounts of money, unbelievable profits, but the world's full of able people, and the question we have to ask ourselves is: if it's so easy for us to make so much profit what's to stop everybody else doing the same?' The answer was there was no impediment. The barriers to entry were very low. So, at that stage, we decided that, now we had so much more capital, we would invest much longer term to produce products in which the barriers to entry were very substantial."

Psion plumped for two areas: one was applications software, the other was pocket computers. Disaster was lurking. Sinclair had asked Psion to do the software for his QL computer – an early SOHO machine. ICL, then the sixth biggest computer company in the world, was also involved. Psion thought that, if it succeeded, they could produce a version for the IBM PC as well. It was a giant project for Psion but their recent acquisition of a DEC VAX minicomputer for development work gave them confidence.

The second major new departure was the portable computer. "It was a unique product. No one had ever thought of it before. It was not a calculator but a computer designed for information management for the individual. That was the genesis of the Psion 1."

Psion developed the QL software and a golden torrent of royalties seemed within their grasp. "We were very wary of Sinclair because we knew the company well, and we thought they were at risk. We thought the same about Acorn – they were a vehicle which had lost control. We knew these companies were not long for this earth.

"I remember going to a party at Clive Sinclair's house in Cambridge – The Stone House – round about 20th December 1984. It was a wonderful party – everybody in the industry was there, there were lights strung up all around, and there was grand food and it was meant to be a celebration of this great success. And it was a great party. But there was an atmosphere about that party where everybody – well not everybody, but certain people – knew that their companies were effectively bankrupt. Some didn't even realise that was the case. Acorn had just been quoted on the stock market and it was bankrupt, as we saw, in January or February. Sinclair died more slowly.

"The QL was launched in early 1984, prematurely as usual, and without all its engineering sorted out. Our software was fantastic. I am very proud of what we did. I remember a journalist writing: 'Psion hits a pot of gold'."

The collapse of the microcomputer market left companies without revenues to pay crippling bills from suppliers. It was made all

the worse because, in previous years, microcomputer makers had
been caught out by the scale of the demand and had not built up
enough stock so, for Christmas 1984, they ordered masses of
stock. "I remember Nigel Searle, who was the managing director
for Clive Sinclair, saying to me: 'Whatever happens we are not
going to run short of stock this year.' He was right. He was
absolutely right!"

The collapse of the microcomputer market meant that the
promised pot of gold eluded Psion. It was made all the worse
because Psion had funded the software's development itself,
banking on the revenue stream from the royalties. So it forfeited
its investment as well as the hoped for royalty stream. "I could
have got Sinclair to say: 'Halve the royalty and we will pay you a
million pounds up front to fund the development.' But we had
more than enough cash to do that ourselves, and on this occasion
we lost."

So, instead of a golden year, Psion had a difficult 1984. Two
things helped to mitigate the pain. In November 1984, Marks &
Spencer approached the company with an internal application for
organisers. Not only did the M&S requirement generate a huge
amount of business, it was the start of Psion's Enterprise Division
which tailored organisers, and their programs, to individual
companies' needs.

The other thing which helped Psion through 1984 was that the
company had negotiated a £1 million equity investment in 1983
from venture capitalists. It had been a salutary experience of the
City's ways. Two venture capital groups had been involved and
Psion discovered that they had got together to drive down the
valuation of Psion in order to get more equity for their money. "I

wasn't negotiating with two companies, effectively I was negotiating with one." Psion ditched them both and went to friends or
'business angels' in today's terminology. The silver lining on the
cloudy year of 1984 was the launch of the product line which
made Psion a household name. Organiser 1 comfortably exceeded its business plan, which was to sell 10,000. Actual sales topped
30,000. But Organiser 1's real importance lay in the lessons Psion
learned from market feedback. Those lessons resulted in Organiser 2. "We developed the software hugely in the Organiser 2. The
software was terrific. The operating system in the Organiser 2 was
the first real EPOC system. It was launched in April 1986. A month
before it was due to ship I was supporting our development
people at 3 am. In a smaller company you're a . . . a . . . wolf
pack, and I was going around giving them burgers, milk shakes,
Cokes and so on and, at about 3 am, Colly (Myers) was working
on testing the software system and he turned to me and said: 'This
thing is going to run.' And it did. The Organiser 2 had more
speed, had much greater capacity, ran like the clappers and had
what we at Psion call charm.

"Charm is a term for software invented by Mitch Kapoor
(founder of Lotus). Charm is very intangible and difficult to
define. We can define functionality, and write it down in a spec,
but there's another aspect to software. Software is not just software; software is a virtual machine. What led to the Industrial
Revolution was the creation of the machine. Now we have virtual machines because software is a machine – a machine which is
hugely more variously applicable with a well-nigh infinity of
levers – which is bringing about a revolution more profound than
the Industrial Revolution.

"People talk about the Internet changing things – about e-commerce – but those are just the latest manifestations of something much wider. What is changing things is the virtual machine which is replacing mechanical systems everywhere we look. It is changing economies. It provides a completely new environment for the way business is carried out. So software is very profound. In many ways, the root of Psion is software.

"The characteristic of software being brilliantly designed in terms of its ergonomics for people is one element of charm. When you look at the screen and say: 'Wow! If I press this button this is probably going to happen,' or if it invites you to try it – if it's intuitive. It's also speed. When you press something it's *schweeeeeet* – you don't sit there – it happens. It's also about reliability and robustness – you press a button and it doesn't crash. Charm defines a set of attributes that are intangible, or difficult to define, but which are profoundly important. And that's why we knew the Organiser 2 was going to run."

Organiser 2 was launched in April 1986 and drove Psion's growth through the second half of the 1980s from a £5 million company to a £30 million company. It was still in production – for industrial use – in 2000. In 1988, Japan struck back. Sharp and Casio of Japan copied the concept, even using the organiser name and publishing advertisements so similar to Psion's that legal action was contemplated. The Japanese expanded the market but took an increasing share of it. "By 1990, the Organiser 2 was pretty long in the tooth. It was beginning to look a bit dated and clunky. The Japanese products were slimmer. We were losing the market.

"We saw this coming, but we had decided not to follow the Japanese practice of incremental improvement. We had two advantages the Japanese didn't have. First, we had a vastly superior understanding and knowledge of software in this field, and second we were actually an IT company, not a consumer electronics company, therefore we had a much better understanding of what was going on in the IT industry as a whole.

"So, instead of evolving the Organiser 2 to Organiser 3, using the same architecture and technology, we decided to jump straight to the environment of the mid-1990s in terms of architecture, chips, screens and office requirements. We decided we had to move from MS-DOS to a Windows-driven, small, robust form-factor system, with pull-down menus and icons."

Psion had started work on the concept in 1987, but didn't launch a consumer product until 1991. "The Japanese ate into our consumer market severely in 1990 and the beginning of 1991, and our turnover went down in 1991 as a result. I remember a journo writing: 'Potter needs to sell the company fast.' The stock market had pushed our valuation down to £10 million. This journo was telling me to sell Psion for £10 million. He didn't know what I knew – which was that we had a very hot product about to come up – the Series 3."

Also pushing down 1991 figures was the hit which Psion took for restructuring Dacom. Psion had bought this "very small, funny, modem company" in 1989, in the belief that "the ultimate estuary of this (Organiser) development would be on-line wireless data machines." In 1989, Psion was valued at £30 million and it had paid £500,000 cash and £3.5 million for Dacom. "The Series 3 had charm. It had 16-bit architecture which gave it huge memory capacity. It had a graphical user interface which was in a completely different league from the Japanese machines. And it had utility – you could take it out of the box and use it immediately whereas with others you had to go off on a course somewhere to learn how to use them."

Psion sold over three million of the Series 3, plus loads of software and peripherals. Growth throughout the 1990s came primarily from the Series 3 and from modems. Toshiba had asked Psion to design a slot-in modem. That was followed by the first-ever PC card modem and Psion became No.1 in Europe in that area. In 1992 Motorola approached Psion to work together on packet-switched data networks and produced an expensive, rather heavy device which was sold to companies and to the Danish police force. But that technology became the enabler for Psion's key focus in the 1990s – adding wireless communications to its products.

Management at Psion was an art to be learned on the fly from friends, rivals and books. "I learnt from Hermann Hauser, from Clive Sinclair and from Roger Foster (of Apricot), and I've always been an avid reader and networker.

"There was a management team, and I discussed things with them, but it's not quite the same thing when you own a large proportion of the company. There is always the sense of responsibility. You've a lot of employees, a lot of suppliers, you've got customers, you got all kinds of responsibilities.

"I've always been the team facilitator. I've never lost any key executives at a high level. The team was always hugely important. I was the strategist, the visionary, but I'm not hands-on. I don't need to call the shots and run everything; whereas Alan Sugar does, and so does Rupert Murdoch. Murdoch has a hundred ideas a week – the problem for others is to rein him in. His executives don't last terribly long, he always finds a way of getting rid of them, which is quite a healthy thing because you're avoiding group-think. I could argue that in the mid-1990s Psion got itself into a habit of group-think, because there was so much loyalty that we were a kind of cabal. It became important to change the team to avoid that."

Conventional business plans are not to his taste. "Anybody can produce a business plan. I can produce a business plan for selling asparagus-flavoured ice cream to Alaskans – and I could probably go and sell it to some venture capitalists. I bet I could do that and raise £5 million!

"You need to be very careful with business plans because they're only as good as the ideas, and the real world is actually not like the idea. The idea is an idealised, theoretical world, and real life ain't like that. What you should really do in a business plan is to describe the merits and advantages of what you're going to do compared to other similar ideas, why you are going to do better than others, and what skill sets and assets you are going to be able to bring to this project that will give you leverage and advantage.

"The second aspect of a business plan should discuss what to do when things go wrong. It should be 'non-linear'. A non-linear business plan recognises that, as you execute the plan, the world is going to change. Things take longer, or move in a different way than the plan. For instance, you'll get some prototype products, and you'll show them to the market, and customers will say they don't like certain things about them and so, instead of launching the product, you'll change it and get it right. You need to learn from the market.

"What I'm saying is that reality – feedback you get from the marketplace and from suppliers – is what you must learn from. If a business plan doesn't take account of that feedback process – the feedback loop – then it is a poor business plan and most business plans are like that. Now feedback in physics or electronics is non-linear – that's what I mean by a non-linear business plan.

"Of course in every business plan we're going to try every which way to make Version 1 a success, but it might turn out to be a great big learning curve. So we're going to build in finance to deal with Version 2 – now that's a business plan which is a bit more clever. After all, Bill Gates said: 'No piece of software works until Version 3'."

Important to business success is judging people. "I'm a good judge of people. I have always been able to appreciate what's the coffee and what's the acorns. It takes me seconds, and 90 per cent of the time I am right. But about 10 to 15 per cent of people I meet are more complex and opaque, and it takes me longer to make judgements on them."

One example of this was a proposal that came from within the company. David didn't know the people who'd put it up, so he went to see them. "My nose twitched from all kinds of smells. They were too easy with answers. When you ask a question, and it's a difficult question, and people give you a facile answer, you are wary of them, because they're trying to hide something, they're trying to skate over to somewhere else, trying to sweep something under the carpet.

"When you meet a new small company you ask: 'What makes them tick? How are they looked at by their peer group? Is this really a team? Or it a couple of wide boys who have managed to cobble something together?'

"A large business is a broad church with a lot of skill sets. Some people are wonderful operators but are not very good in terms of strategy. But if you show them the way and say: 'Off you go Patton – go and hit the Germans from the South' – once he's got that, he'll do it. We've got lots of Pattons.

"Judging people is very important. The experienced business-men I respect all have that ability. But I have many friends who are excellent managers, some of them directors at Psion, who always look at the positive side of people and they're not good at judging things like that. I put that down to the fact that they are nicer people than me.

"It's a game my wife and I play. When we go home from a party we always analyse everyone there. It's a journalistic facili-ty. I think it was Fay Weldon, the writer, who said: 'I never meet anybody at a party who I wouldn't want to follow home and find out what really makes them tick.' I have the same inquisitiveness.

Being a public figure and married to a journalist creates con-tradictory feelings about the press. "The press can be very intrusive. What's appalling is that *Sunday Times* Rich List thing – it's dreadful. It shows a uniquely English kind of prurience. Of course there is a legitimate public interest in matters relating to a public company. But your children have nothing to do with that. And your private house has nothing to do with that. But I'm happy with the media. I've dealt with a lot of journalists for many years, and I give a lot of public lectures, and I'm comfortable doing that."

Psion is a rarity in Britain for making a success from technology. "In scientific terms we are an extraordinarily creative and
advanced culture. The number of citations in scientific papers that
are published per head of the population in Britain is the highest
in the world, while the total number of citations is second only to
the US. So why are we so outstanding in science and so poor in
turning that into something commercially successful?

"I've just finished a year's investigation in the Council of
Science and Technology on this very issue. The answer lies in the
fact that in Britain we have a high regard for science. Science asks
questions about the secrets Nature guards. 'What is matter made
of?' 'What is gravity?' 'Why do apples fall?' We have high regard
and high esteem for the activities associated with finding out
about the things which were not made by man. But we don't have
high regard for understanding the things which are made by man.

"What motivates scientists is curiosity. It's nothing more or less
than that. So why is it that we don't have the same regard for asking questions about things which man makes, as for the things
made by Nature? I think the questions that technologists ask are
just as profound as those which scientists ask.

"Scientific curiosity isn't particularly noble. Scientists are not following some priestly goal to benefit mankind – they're just
motivated by curiosity. It's selfish. There is no great nobility in
curiosity, just as there's no great nobility in making a bigger chip.

"In Britain the science establishment is enormously powerful –
the Royal Society is intertwined into government. When Tony
Blair has a problem he asks the Royal Society and he asks the
Council for Science and Technology – I am one of the few technologists on the Council – it is dominated by scientists.

"Edison personified the value and importance of technologists. Edison is a great hero in America. He used our understanding of sound waves – the work of Boyle and others in the mid 19th century – and he used this to record sounds. It was a rather extraordinary thing when you think about it, because up to then sound was something ephemeral – you couldn't capture it. You listened to it, and it was gone. It wasn't that Edison was motivated by a commercial drive, because at the time there was no commercial market, but once he had discovered the phonogram, people said: 'Wow! Isn't that interesting? Is it possible to apply this?' Eventually some wag in his group came up with the idea of talking dolls. They made these and, in the 1880s, the salons of Paris and London and New York were full of these talking dolls – they were the wonder of the age – you pressed the doll's tummy and it said: 'Hi, I'm Petunia', and people said 'Wow! Isn't that amazing?'

"It took another eighteen years from the invention of the phonogram until a different group of people, which became HMV (His Master's Voice), realised you could use this technology to record the work of great artists and musicians and orchestras and singers. So then the music industry was created. And the benefits and value it has brought to mankind have been huge when you think of all the pleasure that has been created by being able to listen to music.

"What that demonstrates is that there are actually three processes involved in creating new products: first, understanding the science; second, understanding the technology; third, finding an application for commercial benefit. In Britain we have the strange idea that the latter two activities are somehow less than the first.

"In America it's the other way round, and the same in Japan. I think that is why we have not prospered in those other two activities, whereas we have in the first. I don't think that the people who created the internal combustion engine which created the car industry, or the phonogram which produced the music industry, or diagnostic equipment in hospitals which show how to cure ill people, are engaged in activities which are any less important than scientific activity.

"Now, in defence of Britain, I'd say there is something not quite right about America. Every aspect of culture and life in America is driven by business. Whether it's Hollywood, or electing the president, or being a writer or a sportsman, it's all about money. People say: 'Wow! He earned $300 million last year. That makes him the greatest sportsman of all time'."

At the same time: "I'm very proud, happy, delighted that in Psion we've got lots of lots of millionaires running around. I think that's terrific. But I don't think that all of life is about business."

Politically, David's a Blairite capitalist. "Capitalism is about harnessing selfish needs to the benefits of society. That is why capitalism works, whereas the model of Fabian socialism has not worked because it goes against the grain of human nature. Like Blair, I want to make Britain an exciting, challenging leader in the world, not a follower, not a museum. I'm a radical, I'm more comfortable with people who want to change things.

"The money is not actually why one does it. One does it for the same reason as the scientists – out of curiosity and the wish to have an impact upon the world. My family and I are very well provided for. I don't have to work, nor have I had to work for many many years."

In his late fifties, he's preparing to take a back seat. "What I've been doing over recent years is building the people in the organisation who can take it forward, and I think I've achieved that. If I walk away from Psion now, the company is going to move ahead strongly with a team which doesn't rely on me."

His biggest mistake was in not buying Palm, makers of the hugely successful PalmPilot. "I actually had a meeting with them to talk about it. I didn't know about the Pilot – they had it under wraps – I was interested in acquiring Palm because of their software and to build a major development facility in Silicon Valley to straddle the cultures. I was happy to acquire it for a reasonable sum, but they proposed an outrageous sum to me. They chose a very large American company (US Robotics) to get the marketing clout across America, which we might not have been able to provide. It wasn't exactly a mistake, because if I'd known about the Pilot I might have done the deal."

Nor does he regret it. "I have a long-term philosophy of business development. I don't believe you build successful companies overnight. Motorola took 70 years to get to its present size – we have another 50 years to reach their size."

Although rated by the stock exchange along with the high-tech, go-go stocks, he disdains the practice of the dotcoms of hyping a brand for quick returns. "I believe brand comes about from great products and services. Brand in itself is not sufficient. It's about benefit to the customer. Just bombarding customers with an image is something ephemeral. What's better is something enduring."

What will be enduring at Psion? "Its position at the centre of the connected world."

HERMANN HAUSER

Hermann Hauser founded Acorn Computers in 1977, the same year he got his PhD at Cambridge. Seven years later, Acorn was a £100 million company and the *Sunday Times* judged him the 12th richest man in England. He spun ARM off from Acorn and ARM became a FTSE 100 company. He founded the chip company Virata, worth several billion dollars. He started the venture capital company, Amadeus, to back high-tech start-ups and raised £50 million for his first fund. In 2000, he raised £235 million for his second fund – Amadeus II

His first love was go-karts. "I like building things. When I was 13 we built a go-kart. I've never liked working alone, and I built the go-kart with my cousin and my brother. We liked driving the go-kart but, even more, we liked it when it didn't work, because we liked fixing it.

"We had started building soap-boxes – in those days all the kids had soap-boxes on wheels – and our dream was to have one with an engine. Then one day my father remembered that somewhere in the bowels of the building there was an old air pump which the French had left after the war. It had a four-stroke engine and he found it. It was one of those great experiences. Someone said. 'How are we going to start this thing which hasn't run for thirty years or so?' And one of the guys said: 'Why don't you soak a piece of paper in petrol and hold it in front of the air-intake and see if it starts?' And we did and it worked. We knew we had a live engine.

"I spent a few days trying to work out the steering geometry. That's bloody hard because the wheels, when they enter a bend, don't change in parallel – the inner one has to go further than the outer one because the two axles have to meet at the back axle."

Overlaid on the teenager's love of building things was a developing interest in physics. "My curiosity in physics was brought about by my uncle during various wanderings through Austrian mountains where we went for excursions at the weekends. When you go on these mountain walks for hours on end, it gets a bit boring and my uncle – who was the local jeweller and who had a doctorate in Physics – started talking to me about atoms and electrons and how you can actually make gold out of lead by just injecting some more protons. It was absolutely fascinating and I started reading books about atomic physics, then about relativity and quantum physics. I just got the bug.

"It is all counter-intuitive, not something you can get through everyday experience. You had to use your brain a bit. I always liked solving puzzles. I had this very nice experience with my brother. We were driving along the autobahn when the car suddenly stopped. We were both totally silent, but we both knew what we were doing. We were thinking through all the reasons why the car could have stopped. Within a few seconds of each other, we both had the right solution. And we opened the bonnet and fixed it. It's an unusual thing when you're driving down the autobahn and the car stops. It was an interesting riddle to solve."

Although hooked on the physics bug, he still had to convince his father that physics was a better career than joining the family wine business. "There was an interesting pow-wow which my father organised when I told him that I wanted to study physics, and he wanted me to study economics. We had a friend in Vienna who was a lecturer in physics and he was brought in to size me up. He said: 'Hermann seems to be smart enough to make a go of it in physics, and he will have a very satisfying life, very exciting, but I must also tell him that he will never have any money. If he's happy with that, OK. If he studies economics and goes into his father's business, he will be able to drive around in a Mercedes. If he studies physics, he'll have to make do with rather less.' So, at 18 or so, I decided that I would never have any money in my life. My father was very good; he accepted that. He said: 'If that is really what you want to do, do it'."

He studied physics at Vienna University, specialising in gravitational theory. He then studied for a PhD in physically activated chemical reactions at Cambridge University's Cavendish Laboratories. England was a natural choice because, at the age of 15, he had been sent by his father to England to learn English. "My father said to me: 'When I was young, my father sent me to France because French was the important language at that time, but now it is English. So I would like you to learn English.'

He had some brochures of schools and it came down to a choice between Exeter and Cambridge. I knew nothing about either of them, but the Cambridge school had a better starting date – by one day – for me. So I went there for the summer. It was very lucky for me because I really fell in love with the place. Cambridge in the summer is very beautiful and there are many good-looking Swedish girls."

So it was to Cambridge that he went to study for his doctorate. It was there that he got his first experience in computers. "I think I was the first guy to include computer-generated graphics output in his thesis, and I learnt how to programme in Fortran."

For a year after he took his PhD, he lectured at the Cavendish. The following year he started his first company, Acorn Computers. "It was a year in which the BBC ran a programme called 'The Chip'. There was an excitement in the air. The same sort of people that are now excited about the Internet were excited about the microprocessor – they had the same sandals, the same frizzy hair, the same wild ideas. I felt very comfortable with them. I bought myself an Osborne book on microprocessors, read up on them, and was fascinated. There was a feeling that the microprocessor would change the world – and it has. People forget that, pre-1977, there were no personal computers."

It cost £100 to set up Acorn in partnership with Chris Curry who had been working as a salesman for Clive Sinclair. The meeting was pure chance: "He was chasing after the same woman as me." Their motivation to start a company was personal. "At that time it was quite unusual for young people to go out and start a company. If it had cost £1000 we probably wouldn't have done it. But Chris came from an unconventional background – the Clive school – and was willing to give it a try, and I came from a business background.

"My father was an entrepreneur who had set up his own company. If you look at entrepreneurship you see that the family tie seems to be significant. People tend to be more entrepreneurial if their parents have been entrepreneurs."

It was not just his entrepreneurial genes but practical familiarity with business that helped. "In the early days of Acorn I did a lot of price negotiating myself, and I remembered, as a little boy, my father buying grapes in the east of Austria. My father had this negotiating technique. A farmer would come up to him and say:

'We've had an excellent harvest this year, they're only two schillings 20 groschen, and they're the best grapes you'll find anywhere.' My father wouldn't react to this at all, and would just talk about the weather and everything else, and the farmer would say: 'Well, since we've had a long-standing business relationship, and since you come here every year, two schillings is what I would take.' And my father would hardly react, and the farmer would say, 'Well, 180 groschen and not a groschen less.' And my father still said nothing, and the farmer would be fed up with my father, and he would walk away and then my father would speak to him for the first time: 'Did you say 180?' and the guy would turn and they'd start negotiating. I'd be terrified that we'd lose the deal and we would not be able to make any wine that year.

"It was the sort of haggling between two adults that a child is not usually privy to. It showed me the background to negotiation in which there's a lot of posturing. It is not very reasonable, but without the posturing you probably pay the wrong price. It was very helpful in buying memories. There was an enormous amount of haggling. I was chief haggler at Acorn."

To build the Acorn Computer, he went down a different technical route to Sinclair but copied his business model. "At that time Clive had just produced the MK14 computer kit based on a National Semiconductor microprocessor. I thought we could make a much better computer based on the 6502 microprocessor – this was Acorn System 1 – but we totally adopted Clive's mail order business model.

"We made our first £3000 from doing consultancy work for a fruit machine company and, after we'd designed the Acorn System 1, we scraped together all the money we had and spent it on a full page advertisement for the System 1 in *Practical Electronics* – in total confidence that, the day after the ad came out, the cheques would roll in, and we would shovel them into the bank, and buy all the materials we needed to fulfil the orders. And it was no surprise to us that, next morning, these cheques came in piles. More than we'd ever thought.

"We were just selling kits, bare boards for these microprocessor hobby guys – the 'enthuserasts' we used to call them. But Chris had this great marketing idea that if the System 1 had a nice case, it would have market appeal. So we were the first people to advertise a thing called the Acorn Atom with a proper keyboard built into a box, which was very similar to the BBC box later on, and he had a very high quality photograph taken – much higher quality than all the other ads in *Practical Electronics* – and we put out that ad. Next morning the cheques just kept coming in through the door and we shovelled all that money into the bank. It was just amazing. And I must admit we were a little bit delinquent in the delivery because we just couldn't deliver fast enough – we couldn't make them as fast as people gave us the money. We sold 10,000 of those at £200 each."

His role was not in designing the product but in finding the people to do the design. "They called me a 'Hoover of Talent' – I used to go out to the University Microprocessor Group and find out who were the smartest designers and hire them to design our computers. So really, right from the start, I was the person who articulated the vision, and found the people to do the designs. And they were outstanding designs."

What was the vision? "To bring computers to the people. To take something that only existed in air-conditioned rooms, used

only by people in white coats, and make it something everyone
could have."

He firmly believes Acorn's computer was "the best in its cate-
gory in the world". He recalls: "Bill Gates came to see me and
wanted to sell us MS-DOS, and we pointed out to him, quite rightly, that we had an operating system – the BBC operating system –
which was far ahead of his. And we had something which no one
else had at that time – a built-in local area network – the Ethernet.
You might well ask: 'Why is the world not Acorn-compatible?'

"I think if we'd understood at the time that working with partners was important, and establishing standards was important,
then the world might have become Acorn-compatible instead of
IBM-compatible. But we thought that all we had to do was to
keep building better computers."

IBM's computers were widely copied and they became the
world standard. Although Acorn's computers were, in many ways,
technically better than IBM's, they were not copied by other companies and they did not become a world standard. That was a
lesson which paid off when Acorn divested its microprocessor
operation into a separate company called ARM. ARM's strategy
was to find partners. It did, and it has become a global operation.
Nonetheless, one partnership did propel Acorn into the big time
– and it was with a very big partner indeed. "I was doing all the
buying and Chris did all the selling. He was brilliant at it. He was
the one that got the BBC contract. Chris realised the importance
of it, and said: 'We must get this contract.' Then it became the
whole objective of the company."

The BBC contract was the breakthrough for Acorn. "The BBC,
in their wisdom, decided that the time had come to educate the

nation about computers. So they wanted to see six people including Clive Sinclair who told them not to see the other five because
there was no option – it had to be the Z80 – if they looked at any
other computer they would be completely stupid, so stop fooling
around and just get on with the Z80. And, if you know the people
from the BBC at all, that didn't endear Clive to them.

"So the BBC came to us with a specification. Clive had said 'The
specification is irrelevant – you've got to go with the Z80 – that's
the right specification.' But we took their specification very seri-
ously. In fact it was very similar to a design which Steve Furber
(one of Acorn's two microprocessor designers, now Professor of
Computer Science at Manchester University) had on his own
home computer which we were going to base our next computer
on, called the Proton.

"But we hadn't actually built the Proton. It was just a design. It
was on a Monday when they came to see us with the specification, and they were going to come back on the Friday. So I went
to Steven and said: 'Is there any chance we can lash one up by
Friday?' and he said 'No'. So I went to see Sophie Wilson (Acorn's
other microprocessor designer) and said: 'I've just talked to Steven
and he says that, if we try hard, we might get a prototype together by Friday,' and she said: 'Absolutely no way, it's impossible, but
if Steven is willing to do it I'll have a shot at it.' Then I went to
see the fastest gun in the West – Ram Bannajee – a PhD student
who had the reputation of being able to wire up a board faster
than you could call out the connections. More importantly, he did
not make mistakes. It took us two nights to get all the components together, one night for Ram to wire up the board – there
were a thousand wire-ups and he made one mistake – it was

unbelievable – and we started debugging this thing on Wednesday. I made coffee, and kept spirits up, and we worked all through Thursday night, and at 8 am on Friday – with the BBC coming at 10 am – the damn thing didn't work.

"So I changed my role from tea-lady to hot-shot designer and I told them that the reason it didn't work was because we had this umbilical cord between our development system and the prototype and I said: 'We're going to unclip that umbilical cord and then it's going to work.' And it did. And they never forgave me for that.

"So the BBC guys came in, and they could not believe their eyes. They had been working with a company called Newbury Laboratories for two years, and they still didn't have a prototype, and they saw us on a Monday and had a prototype by Friday. They thought this was absolutely marvellous. Then Chris Curry had a model made of what this thing was going to look like, and the combination of us making a prototype very fast, and also having a really sexy-looking model, clinched the BBC contract for us."

The contract was to bring the company to the verge of bankruptcy. "When we got the contract, we went to Ferranti for the chips. Their first batch of chips didn't work and this became national news – there were even questions in the House of Commons about why schools didn't have their BBC Micro."

Because of the delays Acorn had to ask for its first overdraft. "I went to see Mr Knight at NatWest and asked for an overdraft, and he said 'Oh, isn't it jolly good to see these young people start companies', and then he did his due diligence by asking: 'Which college did you go to?' and I pointed out of the window and said

'That one across the road', which was King's College, and he said: 'Oh jolly good', and he gave me £10,000 with no business plan, no nothing. Later I went back and asked for £20,000, then £50,000, and got it with no problem."

But it still wasn't enough to tide Acorn over. "With the Ferranti problem affecting us badly, and being unable to touch the money we had been sent by customers because it was in an escrow account, I went and asked for an overdraft of £1 million."

That set the cat among the pigeons. "All hell was then let loose. £1 million was way over Mr Knight's limit, and it had to go to regional headquarters. They simply couldn't understand it. We were totally over-trading and we had no assets at all. NatWest held a major investigation."

A saviour came in the unlikely shape of Barclay's Bank. "Matthew Bullock of Barclay's, who had been in Silicon Valley and understood how they did things over there, took over our account. Acorn has been with Barclay's ever since, and the next twenty-five companies that I started all banked with Barclay's accounts. Matthew Bullock argued that it wasn't such a risk to give us the money because we had £1.2 million sitting in the escrow account – all we had to do was get the machines made. Then Ferranti fixed the problem, and we didn't go bankrupt."

Although admitting to being 'nervous', the problem didn't weigh heavily on him. One thing that helped was that the only personal money he and Chris Curry had put into Acorn was the original £100 of capital.

"We were so young at the time, this all happened only three years into starting Acorn and we had £100 riding on this. If it had all gone phut it would have been very sad, but we would have done something else. I was biting my nails, but I slept through the night.'

"The BBC Micro series turned out to be very popular – like EastEnders – not just a ten-part series, but three ten-part series. We shipped 100,000 units when the projections were only 12,000." It was the making of Acorn. However, Acorn's management was 'chaotic'. They knew so little about finance that they had to go and ask the BBC if they could increase their prices by £100 per machine to £299 and £399 in order to make a profit. Eventually financial people were brought in and the company was more conventionally managed but, in the early days, he remembers it as 'a magic time'.

"There was tremendous excitement about what we were doing in the company. It was almost a self-organising company, because everyone wanted to succeed. They all knew that Chris and I were totally dedicated to the company. We worked long hours and everyone knew that if they stayed until eight o' clock, which was when I got hungry, they could have a meal off me, because I used to ask anyone who was still there for a meal. They got wise to this because they liked having meals with me, and these meals turned out to be major design sessions.

"Lots of clever aspects of the BBC Micro were decided over dinner. They were great fun, those dinners – the Ethernet was designed during one of them. We had them in the Italian Kitchens just next to the marketplace.

"We managed to build Acorn Computers up into a £100 million company on capital of £100. Acorn Computers is the only company I know, anywhere in the world, which had a capital gain of a million times – every pound we put in became worth one million pounds." The million-fold increase in capital worth took seven years to achieve from forming the company in 1977 to going public in 1984. The experience of transitioning from a PhD physicist to co-owning a £100 million company was 'unbelievable', he says. "We were so young, we accepted it as something that just happened. I remember being on a plane, and opening the *Sunday Times*, and seeing a picture of me smiling back at me, and reading that they'd done a survey and I was the 12th richest guy in Britain. And I thought: 'How did that happen?' But I also remember thinking on that plane: 'Is this the richest I'm ever going to get?' and, until 1999 [with the success of his company Virata], that was the case."

At about the same time that Acorn was making the decision to go public, it was making another decision which was to have more far-reaching effects than its stock exchange launch. But it happened almost on automatic pilot. The company had realised that it needed a new generation of microprocessor – a 16-bit instead of an 8-bit [referring to the size of the chunk of information it could process at a time].

"I asked Intel for the 286 (a 16-bit microprocessor) and they said they were not interested." There were, however, other 16-bit microprocessors, and the job of evaluating them fell to Steve Furber. "We looked at National Semiconductor's and Motorola's but they were too slow," says Steve. The obvious answer was to design their own, but this looked daunting. "The general view was that microprocessors had a certain mystique – they were designed by very special people." says Steve, "I'd never designed a microprocessor, and everything I knew about them I'd learned at the Cambridge University Microprocessor Group where people met to make computers for fun. We knew that it had taken National 200 years of development time to build their 16-bit microprocessor, and Acorn couldn't afford that – we only had 300 people at the time.

"Then we came across the Berkeley RISC (a new type of microprocessor). A group of graduate students had built a microprocessor using only a tiny percentage of the resources used by National. In late 1983 I started working closely with Sophie Wilson who had developed all the versions of BASIC for the BBC Micro. Sophie and I went on a trip to Phoenix to the Western Design Centre [an independent microprocessor design house which designed the 6502]," remembers Steve, "and we found it to be a cottage industry working in a bungalow in a back street. That gave us confidence. Sophie started playing with instruction set design. Our mentality was, 'let's have a go at building a microprocessor'."

The next problem was to persuade the boss. "Hermann was a great guy to work for," says Steve. "If he had confidence in you technically he'd back a crazy idea. Building our own microprocessor was a crazy idea – but he backed it."

"Steve is one of the brightest guys I've ever worked with – he's brilliant," says Hermann, "and when we decided to do a microprocessor on our own I made two great decisions – I gave them two things which National, Intel and Motorola had never given their design teams: the first was no money; the second was no people. The only way they could do it was to keep it really simple."

Steve defined the architecture while Sophie developed the instruction set. "While IBM spent months simulating their instruction sets on large mainframes, Sophie did it all in her brain," remembers Hermann.

At 1pm on April 13th 1984, the first ARM microprocessors arrived back from the manufacturer, Plessey. They were put straight into the development system which was fired up with a tweak or two and, at 3 pm, the screen displayed: 'Hello World, I am ARM'. It was the birth of a microprocessor phenomenon – a chip which did the same amount of work as other 16-bit micro-processors but used one tenth of their transistors, – and consequently one tenth of their electricity – a vital consideration in mobile equipment that has to run off a battery. ARM barely had a chance to do much good for Acorn because Acorn fell into financial problems. "We never had a stock control system because we never had any stock. Everything that we could produce just went straight out the door. We finally solved that. We finally had enough capacity, and had computers coming in by the lorry-load – just as the home computer market collapsed. And then we couldn't turn off the tap, because we had arrangements with our suppliers and these were six-month delivery contracts. This is when Olivetti came in and bailed us out. Otherwise we would have gone under.

"It was quite traumatic. On one day we were always in the *Daily Mail* as the people who can do no wrong – the people with the Midas touch – then the next day we had fallen from the pedestal and screwed up. It was quite a sobering experience but one, with hindsight, I'm quite grateful for. Because I'd just turned 30, I was the 12th richest man in the country, and I was telling my wife I didn't think it was appropriate that I should be doing the washing-up.

"But all that only lasted ten seconds and I was back doing the washing-up. But you do have these outrageous thoughts that things will be different now that you're very rich. I was only the 12th richest guy for a year – maybe it wasn't long enough to get used to it."

He became vice-president for R&D at Olivetti. "I worked for Olivetti for two and a half years and it was one of the finest two and a half years of my life. We did fantastic things including setting up a new research lab here in Cambridge which has now spawned three companies, one of which, Virata, is worth $3 billion. Olivetti has 15 per cent of the company so the value they got out of Virata alone is worth many times more than the money they put into the lab."

During his time at Olivetti, Hermann remained on the board of Acorn. It soon became clear that, if ARM was to become sufficiently widely used to be self-financing, it had to be spun off as a separate organisation. "By the late 1980s it was clear that ARM could only survive outside Acorn and it was fortuitous that Apple wanted its own microprocessor," says Hermann. Apple wanted it for a hand-held, pen-based computer called the Newton. That requirement persuaded Apple into being one of the backers for a new company that would hold all the rights to ARM, which would continue to do the engineering work on the microprocessor and keep it up to date. The company was set up in 1990. Although Apple would use the ARM chip, the idea was that it should be made available, under licence, to anyone who wanted it. The lesson had been learnt at Acorn that, in order to succeed, a product had to succeed on the world stage and, to do that, it had to become a global standard, which meant it had to be used by many companies. So

Apple, led by Robin Saxby, went off in search of partners. The flow of partners progressed slowly from a trickle to a stream and then to a flood as companies appreciated ARM's superior suitability for portable products – a growing trend in the 1990s – and also ARM's business model, which meant companies could use an independently owned microprocessor which wasn't controlled by a rival.

The success of ARM was staggering. Before it was ten years old it had entered the FTSE 100 as the UK's 33rd most valuable company. Two out of every three mobile telephones in the world now use an ARM microprocessor. While ARM went on to staggering success, its parent wilted. Olivetti put conventional management in Acorn, and it continued to make excellent computers, but things were not the same. "Acorn swung a bit too far the other way. It became very well run, but it had no vision, no razzmatazz, no excitement about where to go. That was why Acorn finally fizzled out. Its stake in ARM was such a large part of the Acorn value – in fact it was so much higher than the Acorn value that the value imputed to Acorn was negative."

Eventually a share deal was arranged in which ARM's shares were distributed to Acorn shareholders, effectively ending Acorn's independent corporate existence. The set-top box operation was sold to Pace Microelectronics and the team which developed Acorn's set-top box moved with it. "Acorn had the first digital set-top box in the world, but the management team didn't have the vision, or the natural genes which we had, to bet the company on it. They simply didn't have the balls to do it. They didn't have the belief that it was going to work out and they didn't understand the importance of it. Although I was on the board, I could not convince them this was the right way to go."

Also spun out of the old Acorn shell was a company called Element 14 (E14) which was to develop high-end microprocessors for Asynchronous Digital Subscriber Line (ADSL) chips (which speed up telephone lines).

"The person leading the architectural design at E14 is Sophie Wilson, one of the two designers of the ARM microprocessor. Stan Bowen, now chief executive officer of E14, got hold of the best microprocessor team in Europe after ARM's – the team which did the Chameleon chip at STMicroelectronics – and also prised the ADSL team out of Alcatel [the world's largest manufacturer of telecommunications equipment]."

Hermann's next computer start-up after Acorn was the Active Book Company, which made a pen-based computer called EO, a joint venture with AT&T and Kleiner Perkins. It was a rival to the Apple Newton. But pen computing didn't take off.

"The EO had a big launch in Las Vegas organised by AT&T. The EO had a built-in cellphone which was the first true communicator – we called it the EO Communicator – so everyone was interested in seeing a demonstration. So someone in the audience, with an EO, was going to ring up and send a message to an EO on stage. This was in the early days of cellular telephony and some calls didn't go through. And since we had the world's press there and TV cameras, we went to the AT&T guy and said 'we've really got to make this work.' 'OK boys,' the AT&T guy said, 'we'll shut down Las Vegas for half an hour.' And he did. He shut down the Las Vegas cell phone system and made it possible to only ring one number – and that was the number of this thing on the stage. So we knew this call would go through! Only AT&T could do that."

However, EO flopped. The team that developed it went off to work on what eventually became the PalmPilot, which was a huge success. "Some visions work out and some don't. And there's no telling, at the time, which ones will and which ones won't. By that time I had learnt from Silicon Valley that failure isn't necessarily a bad thing. It's painful but you learn a lot more from your failures than you do from your successes. They make you better next time. And it did exactly that – because the next thing we started was Virata. Virata is now worth $3 billion. It was built on the same model as before, i.e. find the best brains in Cambridge; find a growth market i.e. the ADSL market; build a global team with an outward-looking chief executive officer, an inward-looking chief operating officer who makes sure the chips work, and a Harvard-trained chief financial officer to take the company public. This was not actually the original idea. We were originally going for something else – ATM [Asynchronous Transfer Mode] to the desktop – but that was a total flop. But we managed to continue with the company long enough to allow us to change the strategy quite drastically from ATM switches to ADSL. The reason we were able to do that was because we had some excellent American VCs who stayed with us, and because Oracle invested $10 million in us."

Why does he think Virata succeeded when EO failed? "I seem to live in the future, and always ahead of it, and sometimes it doesn't work out. This time we were ahead of the curve and we got it spot on."

Hermann was making a gradual journey from entrepreneur, to venture fund manager, to business angel to fully fledged venture capitalist. At Olivetti he acted as a fund manager for the company's investments in high technology companies and developed a taste for it. "The starting point was the excitement of starting new companies. Although I wasn't worth £100 million any more, I was still worth enough millions that I could risk spending some of my money investing in other companies. That's how I became a business angel. That's what I was for almost twenty years before I graduated, to become a venture capitalist.

"In the US, the business angel investments are four times the size of the venture capital investments. So having a business angel community which can pump-prime start-ups during their very early phase provides the feeder companies into the venture capital community – because venture capitalists can't spend £100,000 on a company and work with it for two years before you've got anything to show for it. VCs don't have the bandwidth to do it. That's the job of the business angel network.

"You can't have a viable business angel network if you don't have people rich enough to say: 'I will put part of my money into start-ups because I can help these guys because I've done it before'.

"There's an excitement about investing in start-ups. Some people enjoy gardening and seeing roses grow – others enjoy seeing companies grow. And the fact that you can make money on this is not lost on people – it's a very nice side-effect. If you get it right, the financial gains you can make are higher than any other form of investment – at least legal ones.

"The idea for Amadeus started at a dinner which John Jackson, chairman of Celltech, organised in London. I sat next to Anne Glover [now his partner in Amadeus] who was also interested in funding start-ups. We decided to do a few deals together. One was NetChannel which was Internet on the TV, which was a flop; another was NetProducts – which was to make the hardware for NetChannel – which was another flop – in fact, the biggest flop I've had, because I put £2 million of my own money into that and it went south. But, at the same time, I put another £2 million into E-trade UK and sold it for $225 million six months ago – so that paid for the flops.

"We also sold UKOnline successfully to EasyNet, so we made a bit of money there. And I was rather impressed with the way Anne handled that."

A year later he'd decided that he'd like to take the plunge into the venture capitalist business and set about collecting a fund with which to do it. He wanted Anne Glover to be his partner but she didn't agree to it immediately. "Basically Anne played hard to get. Her attitude was: 'Show me the money.' Then Microsoft came along and said: 'We want to give you £10 million of Microsoft money to invest in the Cambridge area.' I told Bill Gates: 'I don't want to run a Microsoft fund but, if you are interested in giving me £5 million, and put £5 million in reserve for yourselves so that together we can put £10 million into UK start-ups, I'd be very happy to do that.' And they said 'Yes'. So they invested in Amadeus."

Why call it Amadeus? "I wanted to call it the Cambridge Technology Fund but Anne said she didn't like the word Cambridge and didn't like the word technology. So I told her: 'Think of a better name.' She came back with fifty from Neptune and Saturn to Jupiter and Amadeus. And because Amadeus had the Austrian connection, and Mozart had good connotations for most people, we went with Amadeus."

As well as the £5 million from Microsoft, Amadeus got £5 million from Gilde, the private equity arm of a Dutch bank, then money from BankAmerica, Deutsche Telekom, France Telecom, Reuters and London Merchant Securities. BankAmerica were then joined by Lazards, Dresdner Kleinwort Benson and the European Investment Fund and a number of rich individuals, mostly Americans.

"Then we did something which is standard in Silicon Valley, but new in the UK, which was to have a side fund to Amadeus where individuals put in a maximum of £100,000 and you build a network of people who are positively disposed towards you.

"Amadeus was very well received. I had over a thousand business plans. We've invested in twenty-four, that's a typical 50:1 ratio for accepted deals versus rejected deals."

Why are so many rejected? "Because most business plans are crap. Most get binned right away."

His criteria for judging a business plan are: "1, There's got to be a real need for that product or service; 2, There's got to be a large market with high growth rate; 3, There has to be at least one star in the team; 4, There has to be defensible [i.e. legally protectable] technology; 5, It has to fit the partnership business model."

In terms of personal qualities he looks for: "Enthusiasm. The fire in the belly. Unless people have a tremendous amount of energy, they will not get over the hiccups there will invariably be." After that come: "A fine brain, business nous, a team-building capability, and a good idea – a good business idea."

For his second fund, Amadeus II (which was closed in the autumn of 2000), he raised £235 million. He believes that now, some forty years after Silicon Valley invented the model, the idea of the venture capital-backed high technology company is beginning to catch on in the UK. But it didn't happen until right at the end of the 1990s. The acceptance of the Silicon Valley model didn't just have to come from the financial community, it also had to come from the technology community.

"The excited, visionary techies with a brilliant idea, but no business experience, now know they'll have a much better chance of success if they get someone with business experience to work with. And the business people, who previously wouldn't touch a start-up with a barge-pole, are now seeing that we made 200 millionaires with ARM, and 100 millionaires with Virata.

"Once this became culturally accepted – that this is what you need to do to succeed – these things then happen very fast. Once you get a consensus in a community, they all do the same thing and, all of a sudden, you get traction. One of the reasons I'm so happy and excited about the 300 millionaires that we've made is that it means there's £300 million coming into Cambridge, which is bigger than any venture capital fund."

So far he has not seen any signs of excessive consumption in the Cambridge area as a result of this new wealth. Although house prices are sky-high, the austere, academic Cambridge tradition has, so far, kept the temptation to be ostentatious at bay. The great value of a number of highly successful rich people in an industrial area is that they will use their wealth to kick-start new ventures – thus providing a self-fulfilling, self-perpetuating cycle of entrepreneurial success funding more entrepreneurial success. That is how Silicon Valley has grown over forty years. The value of a knowledgeable, experienced and, above all, rich base of investors is inestimable.

Hermann sees his role in business as that of the facilitator. He can articulate a vision and enthuse others to buy into the vision; he has the technical understanding to tell the wood from the trees and not be bamboozled by technology issues; and he has the gregarious, conciliatory skills to smooth things out when personal issues arise.

Did he ever had a hero or mentor? "Well, Clive Sinclair was certainly the leading figure of the time and we benefited from his mail order business model. He certainly played an important role. But my father influenced me. He had a convivial leadership style, and I learnt from him about the personnel problems you have in any business – that you can't run roughshod over people, that people have to be respected and handled in the right way. John Doerr [partner at venture capitalists Kleiner Perkins] was someone I admired later on."

The books which have impressed him are: "*In Search of Excellence* [Tom Reders and Robert H. Waterman, HarperCollins Trade, 1995] – which I bought copies of for everyone in Acorn; *Crossing the Chasm* [2nd edn, Geoffrey A. Moore and Regis McKenna, Capstone Publishing, 1999] – how you can get stuck before you get connected with the market, and how making the best product doesn't mean the world will beat a path to your door, and *Inside the Tornado* [Geoffrey A. Moore, Capstone Publishing, 1998] – about how you handle super-growth."

What's given him the most satisfaction in his career? "Launching the business plan competition for the Cambridge Entrepreneurship Centre that I'm helping to build up. Ten minutes before I started my talk, which was about how students from US universities set up incredibly successful new companies, there were 25 people in a lecture hall for 300 and I thought: 'This is not going to work in Cambridge.' But when I started, the hall was packed, there was standing room only, and there was a spirit and feeling in the hall that evening that: 'We can do this too.' We had 300 applicants for 100 places. I've never seen young people in Britain have such a positive attitude towards business, and entrepreneurship, and having a go. I thought that after all these years of blowing the trumpet it's finally having an effect."

He's enthused by the success of the Cambridge Network which gets the local business community together with the university to solve some problems. Twelve hundred companies are involved and it spawned the Cambridge Entrepreneurship Centre which arranges tours by financial analysts and books speakers.

His most important lesson in business was "Realising that, during the Acorn period, even the UK computer market was irrelevant – that this is a global game, and the US is the lead country, and we have to understand what the US is doing. Substantial technology companies have to be successful in Europe, the US and Asia. With Cambridge Silicon Radio, for example, we expect to make a third of our sales in the US, a third in Asia and a third in Europe."

What would he say to Tony Blair? "Halve capital gains tax – there's a well-proven link between start-up activity and the rate of capital gains tax. Also share options should be taxed at the time of the sale of the shares, not at the time of exercising the option, because that is the time people have the money to pay for it. And it should be capital gains tax not income tax. Encourage corporate venturing. I talk to a lot of these big companies about start-ups, and you might as well be talking Chinese. Big US companies like Intel and Cisco have very active corporate venturing arms."

For the young, idealistic physics student who had accepted that he would never have any money in his life, things have taken an unexpected turn. "The last thing I expected was to end up being a banker. I'm really a venture capitalist. The nice thing about being a venture capitalist is that you don't really have to retire. You just do a little less. The value of a venture capitalist is the network of people they have and the experience.

"Things for me are now better even than in the early Acorn days. My ambition after making Acorn a £100 million company was to set up another £100 million company. Never in my wildest dreams did I expect that one of them would be a $10 billion company (ARM) and another would be worth $3 billion (Virata), and that I'd have a whole list of companies in the portfolio with the potential of being $1 billion companies."

ROBIN SAXBY

After twenty years as a designer, salesman and manager in the microchip industry, Robin Saxby accepted an offer to lead a start-up microchip company in Cambridge. In under a decade he had made it the 33rd most valuable company in the UK.

It was a very grand hotel on the shores of a Swiss lake and its ballroom was filled with technologists from every advanced industrial country. Speaking to them was a floppy-haired Englishman in the much-loved uniform of Englishmen – a crumpled grey suit. What he was saying made them wonder if they were being subjected to the English sense of humour. He was telling them that his company would be as big as Intel and Microsoft – the multi-billion dollar leaders of the global high technology industry. At that time, Robin's company had twenty employees and counted its income in thousands of pounds. By the end of that decade his company was worth over £9 billion and was quoted in the FTSE 100 and he was still telling everyone who would listen that his company, ARM, was going to be as big as Intel and Microsoft.

He caught the electronics bug early. "I understood Ohm's Law at the age of eight," he says. Not because he was a precocious swot, but because at that age his cousin gave him an electrical outfit "with valves, buzzers and batteries" for his birthday and he became intrigued. His interest was fuelled when a radio buff neighbour died and left his valves and books to Robin. 'I read them and built some radios."

He soon realised his knowledge was worth money. "At 13 I had my own radio and TV repair business. Dad got the orders in the pub. I cycled round and fixed radios and TVs and got the money. Dad went to the pub one Christmas and one of his friends had a broken TV and wanted it to work for Christmas. I got £25 for that, a phenomenal amount of money, and I learnt something about service."

At 15 he was cycling a twelve mile round-trip every Saturday to work in an army surplus electronics store run by a retired major. The pay was seven shillings and sixpence (37½p) a day. "Once, I was left in charge of the shop when he was away and I quad-rupled turnover."

Robin had stumbled upon that agreeable situation when your hobby makes you money. He was able to buy spares from the major at a discount and use them to repair clients' radios and TVs at a nice profit for himself. "I made a good margin and my cus-tomers got a low price." It was the beginning of his business education. Another benefit was that he saw, early on, all the new products coming out of the industry. In the post-war technology explosion precipitated by the invention of the transistor in 1947, new products of ever-increasing power and sophistication flooded out of the world's top technology companies. "I got all the new transistors," he remembers, "I got my hands on all the new stuff early."

Alongside his growing street-level business savvy, he became excited at the rate of technological innovation. It was a potent mix of enthusiasms and one which has driven many high-tech entrepreneurs to success. He was still in his teens. Then the cousin who had given him his first electrical kit, by now a student doctor at Leeds University, invited him to visit the university for a weekend. "We went to a party at a nurses' hostel. We were there till about 3 am. Next day I had a terrific hangover, but I had learnt something about nurses, and that I liked university life, and that I wanted to study electronics."

That made him decide to do maths, physics and chemistry for his 'A' levels. Curiously he also decided to resume Latin, which he had failed at 'O' level. "I am not an Oxford or Cambridge type, but I thought I might want to go to Oxford or Cambridge and I knew you needed Latin. So in the sixth form I continued with Latin. Then someone gave me some love poetry to translate and I liked that, and started to get good grades."

That taught him a lifelong lesson. "Do what you want to do. Follow your instincts. If people say you have to do this, or have to do that – those are the worst things you can say to anyone. If you hate something, why do it? Life's too short."

At that time, Bangor was the best university in the UK for electronics, and Robin won a place there. However, he'd been brought up in Derbyshire, wanted a change from the countryside and looked instead for a big city university. He plumped for Liverpool. "It was the most with-it city in the UK at the time. It had the biggest reputation abroad of any city in the country. Duke Ellington came to play. He was on a European tour and he chose Liverpool as the only city to play in the UK."

He became president of his university hall of residence. "We had the best dances, and made the most money, and bought every block in our hall a washing machine out of the proceeds from the dances. We had the best colour TV, all the best kit and a very good bar." For him, university life was as much about improving student living conditions as about studies. For his final year he had to write an essay and chose the title 'Colour TV: theory and practice.' Colour TV had just been invented.

On the jobs round, the BBC offered him a job and Racal turned him down. He finally went to Rank Bush Murphy in Chiswick working in R&D. He wanted to go to London for the same reason as he chose Liverpool: for the buzz.

"It was fantastic – we were the first people in the UK to work on solid state [i.e. microchip-based rather than valve-based] colour TVs and I was fortunate enough to be designing chips for them from 1968 to 1972." In fact, he did more than just design the microchips, he designed most of the TV. Fate took a hand when he described designing these microchips at a talk to the Royal Television Society. There were some people from Motorola in the audience and they decided they wanted Robin. "Motorola kept chasing me. They offered me a fantastic salary – £3,000 plus a car and I asked them: 'What's the capital equipment budget for my lab?' And they said: 'You don't need to know that,' and I said: 'I'll take a lower salary but I need the equipment'." He didn't go to Motorola immediately, but left Rank Bush Murphy after four years to join Pye TMC. "I wanted a professional engineering career and thought that consumer electronics was not really professional."

However, when he got to Pye, he had a shock. He soon found that Pye was using less advanced electronics in their professional equipment than Rank Bush Murphy was putting into its consumer goods. This was not at all what he had joined Pye for. Throughout this period, Motorola had been keeping tabs on him. "They kept entertaining me and inviting me to parties." One day, a Motorola executive asked Robin: "What colour do you want your Cortina 2000 GXL?" White with black upholstery was his vision of automobile temptation, which finally prised Robin away from the milk and honey of the laboratory to the outer darkness of salesmanship. "It was traumatic," says Robin. "I was leaving the engineering world for the nasty world of sales people and I didn't have a lot of regard for sales people at that time." Another factor was, he says: "Patti and I were fairly newly married and we had quite a big mortgage."

However, sales wasn't as bad as he expected. "I was more of an applications engineer. When I went to Decca I'd go into the lab, put on my lab coat and help them get their designs to work. I'd literally take the circuit board, and get the oscilloscope out, and help them. For the first year at Motorola I spent 90 per cent of my time doing engineering and actually getting Motorola's products designed. Then came the recession of 1974, and all the customers were going out of business, but I quadrupled my turnover in 1974 compared to 1973 and so I got promoted several times."

In other respects, Robin found the new job rubbing up against his principles. "I was not comfortable with the concept of the price being as much as you can get. I wanted to give a fair price."

In the microchip industry, prices are a moveable feast. When microchips are in short supply, they are expensive. When there's an oversupply, they are cheap. The industry has historically lurched from oversupply to shortage. Instead of selling on the basis of what something cost to make, plus a fair profit, Robin found himself locked into negotiations with buyers in which the "different sides were out to try and do each other."

"There were some real foot-in-the-door salesmen," he remembers. "One boss told me, 'Just close the order, don't worry about it,' but I told him it was the wrong thing to do. My boss told me 'We're short of bookings, get it on the backlog.' So I took the order and six months later we got a cancellation. I learnt to trust my own judgement."

Some colleagues had principles he agreed with, some didn't. It was the same with customers. "So I picked the best and left the rest."

It was a time of self-test. "My innate personal values have held true throughout my life," he says. "The nice thing about business is that we do have some choice about what we do." This choice is important. "The only way to be successful is to do what comes naturally to you." The self-test was only beginning. Life got tougher when he left Motorola in 1984 to take up his first managing directorship at Henderson's Security Division. The group was in acquisition mode at the time and was buying new companies on a regular basis. There, Robin ran into a horror of a manager. One example of how he would bully his subordinates was his meetings trick. "You'd go to a meeting and he wasn't there. Eventually he'd turn up and say 'Didn't my secretary tell you I delayed the meeting by half an hour?'."

Now, he reckons he was lucky to be exposed to such a manager at an early age (he was 37). "It put some steel in me. I'm better and more self-confident now because I had the resilience and energy to bounce back. I know how one can be nasty." There were some positives about the job, the chief one being "doing a CEO's job for real.

"My two years' business practical was a huge learning opportunity," he says. It was made all the richer from getting to know the entrepreneurs who regularly sold their companies to the group. But underneath he was a fish out of water – a lone electronics engineer in a company of mechanical engineers and, when the call came to return to the microchip industry, he answered it. The call came from Jean-Luc Grand-Clement who had started a microchip company with two industry veterans Robb Wilmot (formerly managing director of ICL and Texas Instruments UK) and Bob Heikes, an ex-National Semiconductor executive. Their company had heady ambitions. It was called European Silicon Structures, or ES2 for short. It believed it could make technological breakthroughs in microchip design and manufacturing which together would revolutionise the microchip industry. Software breakthroughs would, thought the founders, allow almost automatic design of microchips, and a new kind of machine (called a direct-write e-beam machine) was expected to make them to order. Forming a microchip company on the basis of making one breakthrough is usually risky enough. Basing it on two breakthroughs is high-wire stuff.

On the other hand, ES2 had some heavyweight financial backers, including Philips of Holland, and British Aerospace, which put in venture capital amounting to $100 million; the founders were highly esteemed in the microchip industry; and the company's technology looked potentially world-beating. It was riskier than Henderson but, never one to shirk risk, Robin joined up. He became managing director of the UK company, president of the US subsidiary, and gained his first experience of doing business in the Far East.

As so often in the high-tech industry, technology advances take longer than first assumed, and sometimes don't happen at all as expected. ES2's breakthrough e-beam machine didn't work as well as it should. The high promise of the new software was not fulfilled. ES2 survived – but by using conventional design and manufacturing techniques rather than the breakthrough ones which had been expected to revolutionise the industry. Instead of being a pioneer, ES2 became a me-too.

It was time to take another call. Among the many that came in was one from a new Cambridge start-up company backed by Apple and Acorn Computers.

"I kept turning down Cambridge start-ups because I thought Cambridge didn't have much business credibility. But when I heard that Apple was involved I became interested, because Apple had been both a technology success and a business success." The potent cocktail of technology and profit – first sampled at the major's army surplus store – guided his judgement.

The job was to head up a team of Acorn's microchip design engineers who wanted to go independent and market the expertise they had gained at Acorn in designing the microchips inside the Acorn computer.

The computer had been successful in the 1980s and had been adopted by the BBC for introducing personal computers to the British public. The microchip designers thought they could sell their expertise to other companies and formed a start-up company, backed by both Acorn and Apple, called Advanced RISC Machines or ARM. Also steering Robin's judgement was a catalyst at ES2 in the form of microchip designer Robert Heaton who had been part of the Acorn microchip design team before joining ES2. "Robert told me that they were the best design team in the UK. And he told them that I was the best person to lead them," says Robin.

The downside to the ARM proposition was that the design team's speciality was microprocessors – the microchip that acts as the controlling brain of a computer or any electronics product – and the number of failed microprocessors in the microchip industry is legion. So, although Acorn and Apple offered him the job, it was a highly risky one to accept. Eleven year-old Katy Saxby, Robin's daughter, decided it for him. When he was agonising over the decision, Katy told him: "I've got a die here. Throw it, and if you get a six, you'll become a millionaire." He threw a six. That sustained him through the next two, very difficult, years. "At the low points, I felt: 'At least I threw that six'."

It was an opportunity to take something started in the UK onto the world stage, and to make some money. "I did feel it was a wealth creation thing. I definitely intended to make some money. I had no increase in salary and the risk was greater. The icing on the cake was the stock options – it was the same for the founding team of engineers."

Selling this advantage to his wife was no doddle. "Patti said: 'Yes – we were going to make money on the ES2 shares!' "

The first thing was to get accepted by the designers. "I was offered the job without meeting the team. I said I'd like to meet them, and we met up in a pub. I said: 'I'm the outsider here, do you want me?' They said 'Yes'."

Most important of all, he had to figure out what the job was. It was by no means clear how he was to create a business out of the raw talents of twelve designers. "The headhunter guy had said: 'It's a great job. Acorn and Apple are going to ship all these parts and all you have to do is collect the royalties. It's dead easy.' But I thought: 'Apple and Acorn aren't going to ship all these parts. I don't believe it'." It was lucky that he didn't. At the time the products into which the design team's chips were mostly going – Acorn's computers and Apple's handheld computer or personal digital assistant (PDA) named Newton – were failing.

If he had sat around waiting for Acorn and Apple to make the chips so popular that licencing fees would roll in, the £1.75 million of venture capital with which the fledgling ARM started off would have dribbled away, and the company would have died. He had to think of some other way to make money. But first came the 'tacky, tedious, boring, nonsense stuff' of renting an office and getting furniture. A converted barn was rented. With some difficulty, suppliers were persuaded to deliver office equipment on credit. That done, he turned his mind to figuring out how to make the company commercially viable.

When Robin got to know the directors – two from Acorn and two from Apple – he realised they each had different ideas about what ARM was supposed to be doing. No one had given any thought to working out, let alone agreeing, a common strategy. "I had assumed that Acorn and Apple had worked out together what the vision was and what they were doing. I assumed they were all on the same wavelength and I was the outsider hired to follow their direction." He was wrong.

Each of his four co-directors had a different agenda. "That complexity took me more than six months to understand and appreciate. I had lunch every quarter with every board member and treated each as an individual and tried to understand them. Then I got the whole picture."

He learnt something from that difficult experience: "don't take anything at face value." Having understood the different expectations involved, he started to devise a strategy. The conventional way of marketing microchips is to find someone to make them and then engage salesmen or distributors to sell them. But this would have been highly risky for such a tiny company. Clearly ARM, with its meagre £1.75 million of seed capital, could not afford a factory to make its microchips – even in those days, microchip factories cost around half a billion dollars.

One alternative would be to sub-contract the manufacturing to another company but that would have meant paying the sub-contractor for the chips before he could sell them, and that would have been a perilous strategy for an under-funded company in the notoriously price-volatile microchip market. Gradually it dawned on Robin that he couldn't do it all alone. He had soaring ambitions for ARM's microprocessors – to make them a world standard – but he realised he'd need outside help to achieve it. 'If we wanted to become a global standard quickly, we needed partners."

The model was that ARM would design microprocessors and licence them to partner companies in return for a licence fee and royalties on each chip sold. One might ask, why should companies use ARM's microprocessors when they could use their own? And the answer is because one company can't generate sufficient economies of scale in a market using just its own microprocessor, yet no company wants to use its rivals' microprocessors because doing so puts them at a disadvantage to the rival.

Because ARM would have no physical product of its own, it wouldn't be competing with its licencees. Companies would be able to use ARM microprocessors knowing that their rivals would be using them on exactly the same terms. So no one got an advantage over the others.

It was a business model that depended on trust, and Robin is a man for inspiring trust. He's an affable, approachable chap with the techie trademark style of entering straight into conversation without much social pleasantry or preamble. He has the open, intellectually challenging, way of the technology industry typified by the "Yes, but . . ." style of discourse which means you're not just exchanging compliments – you're there to get somewhere. If he's interested, it won't be long before he says: "Let's get a beer and talk about this some more."

Essentially, his is an engineer's outlook on life. It's a 'let's get together and figure out a solution' approach. Fortunately, the world's high-tech industry is still run by engineers, probably because it's still too technocentric to be turned over to the MBAs and accountants.

In order to succeed, Robin had to gain the trust of companies operating in every advanced industrial country – notwithstanding differences of culture and business style – and that was a tough call. What helped him to gain that trust was the common culture of engineers and the cosmopolitan nature of the high-tech industry, but it also had a lot to do with him. He's straight, and he comes across as straight.

So ARM became a microchip company with no microchips. It had no factory. No physical product. It became the first company in the microchip industry to sell nothing except intellectual property. The ARM model benefited the electronics industry because a common standard meant that there was a much larger potential customer base for products using an ARM microprocessor than for a microprocessor made by anyone else. That's because once an electronic product had an ARM microprocessor in it then, no matter who manufactured the product, the paying customers in the high street could use it with all the familiar software and features of every other product with an ARM microprocessor in it.

So customers benefited because they found competing products in the high street which were similar to use, while the product manufacturers benefited because standard products, similar to use, would appeal to more people. Standardising products is usually done to make the public feel comfortable with the product. For instance, no one wanted a Betamax video recorder when the world had agreed on VHS for the VCR standard.

The obvious example of how a standard can work is the mobile phone, over half of which, by the end of the 1990s, were made with ARM microprocessors. The technical reason why ARM's microprocessor was suitable for mobile phones was because it was small, inexpensive and used exceptionally little electric power, which made it ideal for portable products relying on batteries. The business reason why ARM's microprocessor was suitable for so wide a variety of different companies' phones was that customers were offerered a wide choice of competing phones, all of which worked in the same basic way. Although the same thing had happened with PCs, standardisation had proved to be less attractive because the standard was based on a microprocessor owned and made by only one microchip manufacturer – Intel. The fact that Intel owned that microprocessor meant that the company could sell it for high prices, which kept the price of PCs artificially high for a decade.

Electronics goods manufacturers never again want to get into the position where they have to rely on one supplier for a microprocessor – or indeed any other component. The PC experience has put them off repeating that situation for a very long time. But ARM's business model ensured that lots of companies could supply the microprocessor so there was plenty of price competition in the market. At the same time, the ARM model made it possible for the mobile phone manufacturers to make standard phones which all worked the same way. They all worked the same way because they were controlled by the same standard microprocessor. But, instead of one company having the right to make the microprocessor which would keep prices high, many companies could make it, which kept prices low. So it was ARM's business plan, just as much as ARM's technology, which helped fuel the world's love affair with the mobile phone. The only problem with Robin's business model, once he had devised it, was that no one at Acorn or Apple liked it. "No one could believe that it would work. We had a lot of debate, discussion and argument at board meetings. I said that the world is changing and that our model was based on where we are going not where we have come from. The power of the model is that it thrives on change."

In the end it took him nine months to get everyone to agree that the partnering approach was the right business model. "The breakthrough came at the third board meeting. We produced a strategy which everyone agreed with. Now we could be left to get on with running the business."

Now, one of Robin's chief regrets about his career at ARM was that it took nine months to agree the strategy. "With hindsight, it should have been done in the first few weeks."

With its course set, the good ship ARM could set sail but it was years before it was out of troubled waters. "It was drama all the way," recalls Robin. "We were not at all sure it was going to work. It was not at all certain we could get anything right, and it was not until 1993 that there was some real hope."

The previous year ARM had narrowly escaped running out of money when it sold a licence to Plessey Semiconductors which had been taken over by GEC (now Marconi). "We concluded the deal in July then it took until January for GEC head office to approve it. That was the way the company was run in those days. It could have happened so late that we'd have run out of money."

As a back-up strategy, in case the Plessey deal fell through, Robin had a new investor lined up – Nippon Investments – gained after almost constant journeying to Japan. "I was going to Japan every month. It was during those lonely hours that life seemed pretty tough."

Then Sharp of Japan took a licence. "On my tenth trip to Japan, Mike Muller came with me and we went to Nara [where Sharp has its HQ] and we saw a Sharp sign and I got Mike to take a picture of me standing under it – for luck."

It worked. Then what really put ARM on the map was Texas Instruments (TI) taking a licence. TI, inventors of the microchip, has been one of the world's leading microchip companies ever since there has been a microchip industry. Having TI as a licencee was a powerful endorsement of ARM's technology and business model. Around that time, another early licensee, Cirrus Logic, signed up. Suddenly, things started to come together. For the first time, significant revenues were beginning to come in. Then Robin realised two things: first, that the business model was going to work and second, that: "I didn't have to do everything myself – I had the money to hire people."

He hired sales and marketing people and some lawyers: "We went quite quickly from 25 people to 100 plus – they were great, fun days."

Suddenly, from working with a group of friends, he was into people management. Traditional, hierarchical top-down management has long proved unproductive in high-tech companies. "Fear doesn't work as well with computer architects as it did with galley slaves," as Intel chairman Andy Grove once put it. ARM had nothing to sell except its intellect and creativity. These could only flourish in an open, egalitarian working environment. It was Robin's task to create and manage one. To do it he had to use all the skills he'd amassed in his career: the microchip design stint which allowed him to understand the sometimes swollen, but often fragile, egos of his techies; his selling experience which made him aware of the high importance of a customer; and the lessons of his managerial career which never allowed him to forget that he had to make the numbers every month.

Internally he had to create the most intellectually stimulating environment possible. "You don't have to have the biggest job title to make the biggest contribution; you have to recognise that the title doesn't matter, it's the contribution that counts and that must be reflected in the stock options," says Robin, "so we have a grading scheme which recognises that senior engineers producing patents are valued as highly as managers. Without patents we don't have a business."

The team had to be coaxed and kicked, criticised and supported. "There are times to criticise people – people can coast – and there are other times when they're working really hard and may have lost it and need support. We have a saying in the company: 'If you haven't made a mistake you're not trying hard enough.' If people have problems and pressures we like to help. At the end of a heavy design – when no one knows whether or not the chip is going to work – then that part of the company comes under pressure; or if negotiations are going badly for a licence, then that part of the company is under pressure. They all get pressure points at different times – so one is up when another is down and we try and help each other."

His early lessons gained from trying to reconcile the different agenda of the ARM directors showed up in his management style of taking nothing at face value, of checking and balancing every input. "If people tell me something and I check it out with their staff – that can cause stress. I tell them that I have to do this to get the complete picture. In life we've always got just a certain amount of information. I have to make judgement calls on certain things. I explain to them: 'I have to get a complete perspective.' I tell them: 'Trust me, this isn't against you; it might be a bit unconventional, it might be painful, but it's better for us if we work it out this way.' I tell them: 'You're entitled to do exactly the same with me. You can check out what I say. I don't mind.' "

He concedes it's a management style that can cause stress and one that some people simply can't get along with. That's when the steel shows. "If I have a manager who doesn't like that then I'd say, for the ARM culture, we've got the wrong manager."

Openness and good communications within the company mean a lot. "People are working on individual projects, and it's important they know that what they're doing fits in with the

overall picture. At an individual level we want people to be thinking all the time: 'Does this fit?' 'Am I doing the right thing?' 'How
is this helping?' It's self-management really."

Openness became more difficult with the public offer. Once a
company is public then giving out information which can affect
the share price can only legally be done under tight restrictions.
'One of our problems, now we're public, is: Can we still tell the
troops what's going on?"

To the world outside the company, Robin had to be a diplomat,
looking after his licensees, who are both his customers and his
partners. He's good at this, maybe because of his boyhood appre-
ciation of customer service, or because of his dislike of aggressive
selling, or as a result of his engineer's 'find a solution' mind-set.
"The classical approach to negotiation is adversarial – the salesman wants a higher price, the buyer wants a lower price,"
he says, "but in today's complex world, it isn't about getting the
lowest price and the highest price – it's how we can work it out
together and how we can do a deal that we both feel very happy
about so we can carry on doing deals over and over again and
grow together.

"There is a path of mutual success here based on the premise
that if you pay me too much you may be reluctant to come back.
I try to find the acceptable deal that works for the long term.
We're all interdependent on each other. What really matters is the
people relationships so that, when you have a problem, you can
pick up a phone to your partner on the other side of the fence
and say 'We've got this problem how can we sort it out?' It can be
about people, staff, a product out too late or too early, about
press, about the law – the satisfying thing is being able to pick up

the phone and say 'You're my partner. I want to talk to you as my partner and as my colleague so that, through communication, something good happens.' "

As a practical example Robin cites an incident in the fall-out from Intel's takeover of the US computer company DEC. DEC was, at the time, an ARM licensee and had worked on developing ARM products. "When DEC was sold to Intel, the boss of DEC said: 'I need your help. I want to assign our licence to Intel.' DEC's staff were leaving and I could easily have picked them up. But the boss of DEC had said to me: 'I want to work with Intel.' I could have picked up those people but I thought: 'This is going against what my partner has asked me to do.' With hindsight I'm glad I did that though, short term, I could have had a financial benefit and, perhaps, all sorts of benefits."

He feels the British don't naturally accept the concept of partnering in business. "The attitude in Britain is that we can win against the world. But the idea that you're winning a battle is wrong. We're in a world trading forum – not a football match. Intel is our partner. TI is our partner. Electronics is an interdependent business."

An important skill he has learnt to hone is appreciating people – both recruits and outsiders. "It's a valuable skill to know who you can work with and who you can't. One thing that helps is being very direct. If you're not being straight with me while I'm being straight with you – and you carry on not being straight – that sends some pretty negative signals to me. A certain type of person will come into the room, take charge, make a lot of noise. A lot of people in business are like that – egocentric, with a high opinion of themselves.

"I look for honesty and integrity. I look to see if people listen as well as talk. Some people appear to be listening and don't hear a word. Some people appear to be talking but they're not saying a lot. When people come for interviews I ask all my staff what they think – some people will come in and be rude to the receptionist.

"Personality is very important." He asks himself two key questions: 'Do they fit in?' and 'Do they add value?'

With the new millennium Robin re-set the vision. "I feel we are in start-up mode again. Now we have things we didn't have at the original start-up – a huge patent portfolio, 37 major semi-conductor partners, working relationships with Microsoft and Symbian, and we're No. 33 in the FTSE 100."

As ever, Robin's vision is startlingly ambitious. "We want ARM to be the major influence of the digital age. By 2010 we want to have ARM technology in everything digital, so that every digital product on the planet will have some ARM technology buried in it somewhere."

The strategy for getting there has been drawn up. "We've identified eight key market segments and have people drawing up business plans for each one and what we'll see happening between now and 2010 is different volumes kicking in as different segments have different times to market.

"If we achieve this plan we'll be as significant as Intel or Motorola by 2010. It requires us to have displaced all those Motorola 68000s and 8051s and Hitachis [rival microprocessor brands]. So, instead of everyone designing competitive micro-processors we want them to be licensing ARM. And all these things with ARM microprocessors will be running ARM software.

"By 2010 I'd like every consumer to know that, if they see the ARM logo on a product, it's got better battery life, it goes faster and it has better sound quality, and I'd like everyone with an ARM-powered device to be able to buy ARM software that runs on that ARM-powered device through the Web." He feels that the vision is within ARM's grasp. "If we satisfy our partners and continue to innovate, if we manage our partnership programme well, and listen well, and don't get arrogant, then we can get as big as Microsoft or Intel."

It's the same business principle of marrying advancing technology with a good business model that was learnt by the boy cycling around his father's pub cronies mending their TV sets. The boy's customers are now some of the greatest companies in the world's largest industry. In 1990 he took over a brand new company with no business plan and no direction. By 2000, the company was worth over £9 billion. That's a lot of value to create in a decade and, he says, he's only just started.

To give back something of what he has earned from the industry, he gave £1.5 million to his old university – Liverpool – where The Robin Saxby Laboratory is now established. He holds a visiting professorship at the university, gives periodic lectures there and has been awarded an honorary doctorate.

JORMA OLLILA

In the 1990s, Jorma Ollila transformed Nokia from a sprawling conglomerate with an unprofitable mobile phone division into the world's No.1 mobile telephony company valued at around $200 billion, with highly profitable annual sales of $30 billion, and a reputation for being one of the best managed high-tech companies in the world.

In 1990 Jorma Ollila was put in charge of Nokia's mobile phone business with a brief to decide whether it was worth investing in, or whether it should be sold off. Ten years later, Nokia was the fifth most valuable brand name on the planet with nearly 30 per cent world market share for mobile phones, $30 billion of annual revenues growing at 100 per cent a year, and a market capitalisation of about $200 billion.

In reaching this position, it became one of the world's most admired companies, alongside Microsoft, GE, Intel and IBM. Between 1995 and 2000, Nokia's shares soared 2,300 per cent. This was growth on the scale of a Cisco Systems. In its explosive rise, Nokia humbled the long-time No. 1 in mobile phones – Motorola – which had enjoyed a 40 per cent market share in its glory days, and pushed its Scandinavian rival Ericsson into an unprofitable third place in the handset market.

How did it happen?

"In 1990, the mobile phone business at Nokia was the world No. 2, but it had not been profitable for three years," says Ollila.

Ollila, the newly appointed president of Nokia's mobile phone division, identified two fundamental problems – and one huge opportunity. One of the problems was the lack of manufacturing volume. "The business had huge growth but we did not have sufficient volume to make it profitable," he says. The second problem was the lack of a recognisable brand name. Until then Nokia had been acting almost as a contract manufacturer, producing phones which other people – such as cellular phone operators and the US firm Radio Shack – attached their names to. It had one brand name – Mobira – which did not have a high profile outside Scandinavia. 'We had tremendous problems in our ability to market a uniform brand globally."

The big opportunity was the emergence of GSM as a digital mobile phone standard set to replace the analogue standard in many countries of the world. Having identified the problems and set the strategy, Ollila's execution seems to have been flawless.

First, Ollila sold off many of the other businesses in the group, some of which, such as paper and rubber goods, had been Nokia product lines since the company's founding in 1865. Other businesses to go were the cable business, the power generation business, the tyres business and the TV and computer businesses. The message going out to the workforce – and to the world – was: 'We're in telecommunications, we're high value-added, focused and global.'

The money raised from divestments was ploughed into factories and into engineering. The factory investment was designed to get volumes up to critical mass, so that Nokia could supply globally, the engineering was aimed at making mobile phone handsets more attractive – smaller, lighter, with longer battery life and bigger screens, easier-to-use and better looking than rivals' handsets.

The second plank in the strategy was to establish the Nokia name as a globally recognised and respected brand. Here Ollila unleashed his people's creativity. "Nokia," he says, "is a meritocracy where you can think unconventionally."

Nokia phones started to become noticed, not just because they were technically better than the competition but because they were more 'touch-feely' than competitors' phones. Ollila recognised early on that a phone – to the consumer – was not the same thing as it was to the engineer. Engineers want a feature-rich, technical product; the consumer wants something that works perfectly, is easy to use and seems friendly and intuitive. Ollila also recognised, before anyone else, that the mobile phone was to become a fashion accessory – a means by which owners could express their individuality. Nokia was the first to introduce exchangeable colours for its phones, and was the first to introduce a variety of ring tones.

An example of its very different thinking to its engineering-driven competitors was its 1998 Zippo-style phone. The Zippo lighter is a cult product throughout the world, and Nokia came up with a mobile phone aimed at well-off people. It was sheathed in shiny steel and had the shape, look and feel of a Zippo lighter. When it came out it commanded a fancy price tag – $950.

In the autumn of 2000, Nokia's 3390 model allowed you to customise its ring tone – for instance, with your school song – or customise your screen saver – for example, with a personal photo or logo – and you could programme reminder calls for birthdays, anniversaries etc. "Nokia pioneered the evolution of the mobile phone as a personal, stylish accessory," says Nokia vice-president Rich Geruson, quite justifiably. That's not to say the company gives fashion a higher priority than engineering. The combined computer–mobile phone product, the Nokia Communicator, won the admiration of technologists everywhere who could not figure out how Nokia had managed to prevent the high frequency radio part of the product from interfering with the low voltage, delicate circuitry of the computing side. Engineers all over the world admired that product, because they could appreciate how difficult it was to make.

Ollila sums up his attitude to establishing the Nokia brand as being more than just about the company's products. "It's about the way the company operates, the corporate culture, the company's values."

It wasn't just advertising agencies that were to establish the brand. Nokia people, attending conferences and industry gatherings, tended to be youthful, challenging, humorous and open about the company and its goals. That helped to establish the company's brand, first in the high-tech industry, and then in the public perception.

A sign of a healthily functioning high-tech company is when its people have no fear of talking about the company to outsiders. Ollila's management strategy has been to transmit to Nokia people the company's values and goals, and they come across as people who have internalised and bought into them. Whereas, in many companies, middle and junior people are often shy, or afraid of talking about company strategy, at Nokia it seems to be as natural for them as talking about the weather. In that respect, as in many others, the company shares the Silicon Valley culture established by Gordon Moore and Robert Noyce at Fairchild Semi-conductor and the early Intel.

Nokia became established in the 1990s as one of the world's most valuable brand names. So successful was Ollila's strategy in establishing it that, by the end of the 1990s, a Finnish official noted that Nokia was a better known name in the outside world than it was in Finland. At the same time as he was beefing up the manufacturing, and establishing the Nokia brand, the third plank in Ollila's strategy in 1990 was, while still making phones that worked on various standards, to pursue a major breakthrough with the GSM digital standard. GSM represented a major technological change in the industry and Ollila was astute enough to recognise, as others have before him, that technological change equals market opportunity.

Now Motorola is sufficiently chastened to publicly admit that it was too late to see the switch from analogue to digital technology and react to it. "We underestimated the speed of change from analogue to digital. We have been working hard to remedy that," admitted Fred Tucker, former president of Motorola Semi-conductors, in the summer of 2000.

At Motorola, a company of engineers faltered over the technological transition, but at Nokia, Ollila, a banker, did not hesitate. "Nokia was a challenger in the early 1990s, which meant we had very little historical baggage. The key driver here was 'Go for Growth'. This attitude was already inbuilt in the Nokia culture. To define your growth markets, there had to be a fit between the culture of the company, the core competencies and the chosen area of focus. When we made our analysis at Nokia, our competencies lay in mobile phones and telecom infrastructure. With this kind of fit, we were able to make our choice."

So he pumped resources into R&D for GSM phones. It was not easy. His engineering departments complained about the difficulties involved in implementing the GSM standard, and the expense incurred. "There was disillusionment with the GSM specification," he says, "and there was a lot of pain." Despite the nightmares, he kept the project on track because: "We believed in digital."

He had sound commercial reasons for doing so. GSM was going to be a Europe-wide standard. In addition many Asian, African and Arabian countries had adopted the standard. Ollila could see the opportunity to manufacture phones with economies of scale the like of which had never been possible before.

The GSM network came into use in 1991, with the first ever GSM phone call being made on a Nokia telephone, by the prime minister of Finland. Even Ollila, the apostle of GSM, had not foreseen just how huge the demand for GSM phones was going to be. "The growth was much faster than anything we could ever have imagined," he says. "In 1992 we projected that, in 1999, the mobile phone market, in units, would be around 40 million worldwide. The analysts thought we were too aggressive. We were both wrong. In 1999, the market exceeded 250 million units."

Seeking further economies of scale, Nokia then went for a product range, called the 2100, which had identical phones that worked on the GSM standard, on the US TDMA standard (later CDMA became more prevalent in the US) and on the Japanese PDS system.

In 1993, when the company first shipped this phone, it had projected that sales would hit 400,000. They sold 20 million. Nokia was on its way.

Towards the latter part of 2000, when Nokia was producing sparkling results while Ericsson and Motorola wilted, one financial analyst wrote: "Nokia is crushing the competition. Nokia does the same things cheaper, smaller, easier. In that respect Ericsson and Motorola are at least a design cycle behind."

The outside world perceived Ollila as the saviour of Nokia. In fact he worked closely with a team of people of around his own age in devising the strategy and direction. For the high-tech world, especially the Americans, it all came as a massive shock. An unknown company, from an unknown country, was eating their lunch. Suddenly people all over the world were asking: What is Nokia, and who is Jorma Ollila?

Ollila had been spotted early as a potential high-flyer, winning a scholarship at the age of 17 to Atlantic College in Wales. The college was set up by Outward Bound founder Kurt Hahn to bring together future world leaders from around the globe. "My Atlantic College experience gave me a totally different perspective on world affairs. In practical terms I learnt to be comfortable with foreign cultures, travelling and facing tough challenges. It also directed me towards a career with an international perspective right from the early days of my professional life."

Although prodigiously bright, his main interest as a teenager was ornithology, and he ran the Nature Club at school. The countryside is very important to him – he was brought up in a small town on the Finnish coast where he was born in 1950, the oldest of five children. He graduated with a Masters degree in political science from the University of Helsinki in 1976, then attended the London School of Economics where he was awarded a Masters degree in economics in 1978. He then took a Masters degree in engineering at the Helsinki University of Technology. His first job was at Citibank in London where he worked as a corporate banker for two years, finding it a valuable induction into the ways of business life: "because you learn to analyse the risks of industry."

He must have shone because, two years later, he was on the board of management of Citibank Helsinki. From there, in 1985, he joined Nokia, and soon became vice-president of finance.

Why did he make the switch from banking to industry? "Well, at that time there were tremendous strengths already at Nokia. There was the strength of the culture. We did not have, and do not have today, a bureaucratic culture. Also, people wanted to work for Nokia – there was, and is, an environment at Nokia that allows people to get things done. And by operating in a decentralised way, we actually had many 'pockets' of very good culture throughout the organisation. I felt that there was a determination at Nokia to do well."

It was in 1990 that the big test of his career came – he was made president of the mobile phone division. At that time, the mobile phone division was just one division of many in a sprawling 135-year-old industrial conglomerate which had been based on logging and had diversified widely over the years.

NMTS, the Nordic Mobile Telephone System, had been cooperatively developed by the Scandinavian countries to overcome their geographical problems, so it was only natural that Scandinavian companies should look to provide the hardware for the service.

But while the region developed considerable expertise in the technology, and learnt the importance of working together cooperatively to establish standards and define directions, companies were not, in 1990, finding that manufacturing the hardware for mobile telephony was a profitable activity.

So Ollila's bet on GSM was by no means an obvious one. However, having reported to the board that the mobile phone business was worth keeping – and managing to persuade them of the case for increasing their investment in it – Ollila then had to deliver GSM products. This turned out to be much more difficult than anticipated. The GSM standard had not been defined by Nokia alone, but by the national telecommunications network operators of thirteen different European countries plus Cellnet, Vodafone and the industry in general. As such, it was a hybrid creation, born of compromise and negotiation. Implementing it in practice turned out to be a major challenge.

With all the difficulties involved, it was a major achievement by Nokia's engineers to get working products into the market in 1991.

Ollila was driven by his perception of the exceptional opportunity. "From the outset we believed we were involved in something big. We were always very ambitious, setting extremely high targets for ourselves, and these targets were considered wildly aggressive by industry analysts, even laughable in their magnitude. Ironically, in the end, even we underestimated the size of the market. I think the scope in which mobility has touched and will touch all our lives is bigger than anyone could ever have imagined."

When it was clear that the company was shipping GSM handsets, and that the market was growing explosively, the board of Nokia appointed Ollila CEO of the entire company. That was in 1992, and that was when he committed Nokia totally to the mobile phone business, selling off the other divisions to raise money to finance the necessary investment in factories and R&D which would fund

Nokia's transformation into a global telecoms player. His job, as he saw it, was to build a new company with new morale.

Two years after he became CEO he launched Nokia on the New York Stock Exchange. It was Nokia's rite of passage into the big league of international telecommunications companies. "The telecommunication equipment market is global, its products are global, our competitors are global, so we need global access to capital." Alongside its role in the mobile phone business, Nokia had also become an important supplier of GSM infrastructure. Throughout the 1990s Ollila has kept the company on its basic track of producing user-friendly, easy-to-use, attractive phones, with the aim of extending its market share. It has been said of Nokia's business style that it: "combines the design sense of Apple with the no-nonsense business sense of Cisco."

Ollila has proved to be a leader in the style of the new school – against hierarchies and corporate status symbols. As well as being in tune with the best Silicon Valley practices, this no-frills approach to management appeals to Finns, who hold little respect for author-ity just because it is authority. The country's history of constant warring with a vastly larger neighbour – Russia – has helped pro-duce a flexible national character that is unimpressed by outward and visible signs of status or by dirigiste management styles.

Decision-making is devolved to the people who are best qualified to make the decisions. That largely leaves product development and marketing to find their own ways in a kind of benevolent anarchy tempered by the discipline of budgets and making the figures. New recruits are told to fit into an interlocking matrix of relationships rather than any kind of formal reporting structure of the traditional 'family tree' type.

Nokia's attitude to its 60,000 employees is very similar to how Robert Noyce and Gordon Moore explained the early Intel structure, or rather lack of structure, to new recruits. One recruit joining Intel in the 1970s recalls asking Noyce what the reporting structure was and having Noyce draw a circle with spokes like a bicycle wheel. Noyce put an X in the middle and names like Bob, Gordon, Andy and others around the circumference and explained that the recruit was X, and the names round the outside were the people with whom X might have to interact in the course of getting his job done.

Nokia's thinking is much the same. "You have to figure out a network of people to get things done," according to a Nokia HR manager. It's a way of making the the job the centre of the organisation's focus and pushing inessentials to the periphery.

The intention at 1970s Intel – as it is at Nokia today – was to encourage free-thinking and creativity and promote entrepreneurship, personal responsibility and innovation. Ollila is totally committed to innovation and bringing out new models and types of phone. "You have to innovate all the time, renew yourself all the time," he says. For instance, seven new handset models were launched in the third quarter of 2000. 'Renewing yourself all the time' means that Ollila is strongly against people being able to snuggle down in a comfort zone, and he regularly rousts even his senior managers about, getting them to switch jobs.

For instance, in July 1998, in a roustaround at the very top of the company, Ollila switched his chief US executive into becoming Nokia's chief financial officer based in Helsinki; he called back his chief Asia executive to take on the job of heading up infrastructure development; and he shifted the president of the handset business,

Pekka Ala-Pietila, into taking a central role as his deputy, and subsequently to being president. Although all those involved belonged to the small group of Finns who have worked closely with Ollila in reinventing Nokia, he still has no compunction in moving them around. He says he'd move himself around if he could.

Although he doesn't like seeing people get too comfortable, he is strongly averse to firing people. He says he refuses to see mistakes as disasters, preferring to view them as learning opportunities. "I prefer to use the word 'challenges' rather than say 'not satisfied'. Nokia is a place where we encourage entrepreneurs and risk-takers, a place where you are allowed to make mistakes. Furthermore, if mistakes are made early enough we can learn from them, and even turn them around to our advantage."

He's keen to promote the company to the young as a good place to work. "Personally, I have found that what young people really want is freedom, freedom to make their own decisions and plan their own projects. But at the same time what they also want is to be part of a team, part of a successful team. At Nokia we try to create an environment where this dichotomy is made possible."

Nokia has developed its own internal entrepreneurial process as a way of getting new technologies out of the R&D labs, using the same team which developed the technology in the lab and setting them up as a business unit to commercialise it. An example was 'Smart Traffic' which feeds navigational and other information to motor vehicles.

Although often compared to Intel and Microsoft in terms of scale of achievement, Nokia is different from them in that, instead of relying on a proprietary intellectual property position, it has boldly sought to outrun competitors by making more popular phones than its rivals, relying on open-systems standards.

Ollila has been notably open to cooperative agreements with other companies. Examples are the Symbian joint venture to develop Psion's operating system, EPOC, as the basis for next-generation wireless data exchange; the MeT initiative with rivals Ericsson, Siemens and Motorola to develop security for mobile networks; the Location Interoperability Forum (LIG) to offer location-based services; and a joint deal with Cable & Wireless to provide a mobile Internet platform for next-generation ISPs (Internet Service Providers) and ASPs (Application Service Providers).

There are a host of other similar link-ups. Ollila has shown he believes that cooperation with his market rivals is the best way of expanding the overall market. From that process everyone benefits, and the companies that work best benefit the most.

Giving him the confidence to coexist and cooperate with rivals in establishing common platforms and standards to expand the market is Ollila's belief that Nokia can out-design, out-manufacture and out-market the opposition. Nokia has a fearsome reputation for execution.

Another reason for Ollila's belief that cooperating with rivals is the best way to go is his faith in the boundless potential of mobile phones. In the same way as he saw the huge technological and market opportunities of GSM before anyone else, Ollila is now betting heavily on his vision of the future. "Voice will go wireless," he says. "By 2003/4 the majority of the telephone calls we'll be making will be made over a wireless connection, using a mobile phone. Increasingly the phone will allow you access to data – the Internet, stock exchange information and weather reports."

From 400 million mobile phones sold in 2000, Ollila expects to see 550 million phones sold in 2001, with Nokia aiming to increase its market share. Nokia reckons that global phone market penetration reached 10 per cent of the world's population in 2000 with 700 million subscribers.

Ollila is set on increasing market share because it looks as if sheer demographics will have to slow the 60 per cent annual growth in handset sales between 1995 and 2000. US analysts IC Insights point out that the 60 per cent plus growth rates of 1995–2000 could slow to half that in 2000–2003 simply because, on current growth trends, there would be more handsets made in the world than there are people by 2006.

However, Ollila's vision for the future of the mobile phone is that people will own more than one each. The reason for that is that, while at the top end, people may only own one sophisticated mobile computing/Internet access device, at the bottom end cellular phones will become incorporated into a whole range of different products. Examples are wristwatches or bracelets for plain voice-only use, or phones incorporated into household appliances so that people can dial them up and activate them from a distant location, or in motor vehicles so you can track where they are.

This is because it's now becoming very cheap to make a voice-only cellular phone, and it need take up very little space. In a year or two, a phone's electronics will fit into a single silicon chip – about one centimetre square – costing $10 to make. So these tiny, cheap phones will become ubiquitous – scattered around inside a myriad of different consumer products. These tiny phones will also be invisible to their owner and will simply be a way of tracking your car if it's stolen, or of turning on the CCTV outside your house when you're away from home to see if everything's OK.

That is one reason why Ollila sees people owning more than one cellular phone in the future. They could, in fact, own dozens. The other reason is the high replacement rate. In 2000, mobile phone subscribers were replacing their handsets, on average, every two years. This replacement rate is accelerating. Largely it is due to Ollila's strategy of treating the handset as a fashion item and persuading the young that it's as cool to keep changing your handset as it is to buy new clothes.

Executives from PC companies bemoan the fact that they can't persuade their customers to adopt new models of computer at the same rate as people adopt new models of mobile phone. This is why Ollila drives his people to design innovative and creative new phones and launch new models at an ever-increasing rate. These forces of fashion and innovation – largely conceived and driven by Nokia – are part of the reason why the projections of mobile phone unit growth are so astonishingly high. The other part of the reason is the growing capability of the networks them-selves. As the networks become able to carry more and more data – measured in kilobits or megabits per second – the top end of the mobile phone market will be looking at using the new net-work capabilities to add new applications and uses to mobile handsets. Ollila's vision for the top end of the mobile phone busi-ness is that it will transform into a mobile data terminal. "Mobile devices will display travel information with which a user can keep himself informed of up-to-the-minute changes in train or airline departures. The device will know exactly where you are and give you the appropriate information for that locale. By adding mobility to the Internet we see a great possibility to further enrich peoples' lives and the efficiency of companies. Corporations will benefit from huge advances in productivity."

Pertti Korhonen, senior vice-president for global operations, logistics and sourcing at Nokia, argues: "Work is no longer a place. There will be more handsets than PCs connected to the Net by the end of 2003, putting the Net in everyone's pocket. We are moving towards a phone-centric mobile information society."

However, the Nokia vision of the future is by no means a foregone conclusion. "Who," once asked a disdainful Sir Alan Sugar, chairman of consumer electronics giant Amstrad, "wants to send e-mails from the middle of a field?" At the same time Vodafone, the world's largest mobile telecommunications network operator, is also sceptical about the 'Internet in your pocket' scenario. "The last thing people want is wireless Internet. What people want is information, entertainment and e-commerce," says Tim Harrabin, Vodafone's strategic director.

Vodafone reckons that the key future application is the ability to send and receive video. The examples Vodafone suggests are a surveyor videoing a fault in a building back to his office for analysis, or a paramedic at a disaster site sending images of injuries to a doctor or specialist for advice. The company has also signed up the football team Manchester United to provide re-runs of goals from their matches.

Operators are racking their brains for new services. Some that have been suggested are a service that tells you where the nearest supermarket, petrol station or other facility is, with directions how to get there; a dating service telling you if another subscriber who fits your profile is nearby; and a service linked to Webcams around all the motorways so you can see what traffic conditions are like.

According to a survey in 2000 by the UK Consumers Association, although half the people who want mobile data services want them for e-mail, 20 per cent said they didn't want mobile data services at all. On the other hand, Merill Lynch predicted in mid-2000 that wireless Internet will generate $21 billion in voice and data revenues by 2005, and $32 billion from m-commerce (commerce via a mobile phone).

The greatest example of the success of mobile data services is the experience of NTT's wireless Internet service in Japan, DoCoMo, which had signed up 20 million subscribers by the end of 2000. But no one can be certain that this success will be repeated elsewhere. Many people point to the very long railways commutes which are common in Japan, an ideal environment for accessing the news wires, games and information services provided by DoCoMo. The greatest evidence of apathy towards mobile data services was demonstrated by the poor reception consumers gave the 2000 launch of the WAP service.

So Ollila's faith in the future of mobile data services is by no means a consensus view or a foregone conclusion. It is, nonetheless, something to which he has committed Nokia, in the same way he committed it to GSM a decade ago. The reason for the bet now is the same as it was in 1990: a change in the technology. The current technological change is an increase in the carrying capacity of networks.

At the moment, the data carrying capacity of GSM is very small – 9.6 kilobits of data per second, which is sufficient for voice and 40-word messages but not much more. However, a change in the technology from circuit-switching to packet-switching makes possible some considerable improvements in the carrying capacity.

About a third of Nokia's revenues come from supplying network infrastructure and, sometimes, complete operating networks. For instance, it had the new generation of GPRS (General Packet Switched Radio Services) networks up and running in China, Australia, Switzerland and Taiwan in 2000, and had delivered core networks to over 50 operators, giving it the largest installed base of GPRS networks of any supplier.

As well as GPRS there are two other GSM enhancement technologies (collectively known as 2.5G) which may be deployed to boost network capabilities: HSCSD (High Speed Circuit Switched Data) and Edge. HSCSD offers data rates of 57.6 kilobits per second rising to 115 kilobits per second; GPRS offers up to 384 kilobits per second; and Edge, being developed by Nokia and Ericsson for possible deployment in 2001, could deliver data rates of up to 384 kilobits per second.

Finally, expected some time around 2003/4 is the Third Generation (3G) service which delivers data at two megabits per second – allowing video for the first time.

Ollila is more interested in the market than the underlying technologies. "The customer does not care about the technologies. It's all about giving users interesting and easy-to-use new opportunities." His advice to government is simple: "There are three things that will decide how any society can best work for the common good – education, education and education. And this applies to both developed and developing countries."

For Ollila, the prophet and evangelist of the mobile phone, the future is clear: "We feel like we are changing the world. In the future, people will look back and say this was the time the mobile information age was born."

PASQUALE PISTORIO

B orn in a village in Sicily, Pasquale Pistorio has become one of Europe's best known businessmen. After climbing the Motorola corporate ladder he returned to Italy in 1980 to take up the presidency of SGS, a chip company with annual sales of around $100 million but one that was chronically loss-making. Now renamed STMicroelectronics, the company is the seventh largest chip company in the world, highly profitable, and enjoyed revenues of over $8 billion in 2000.

Pasquale grew up quickly. He was born in 1936 and the Second World War took its toll on his family. "Before the war my father was a trader – buying and selling grain – as my grandfather had done. During the Second World War a big devaluation of the lira wiped out his capital. So, after the war, my father became a government employee, buying and selling grain for the government in order to moderate the market price, and give some incentive to the farmers.

"My father was not paid a salary but a percentage of the grain that was stored. In order to support his family and enjoy a good standard of living, it was necessary to have two stores, and these could not be in the same place – they were 18 kilometres apart. My father could not run both stores and so, during our school vacation, me and my brother started helping my father in his job – I was thirteen and my brother was ten.

"It was run in a good family spirit and I learned the importance of contributing to work. To be available for the grain season, I would finish school a little bit early and start a little bit late. This work, and helping my father, gave me great pride and a sense of responsibility."

He remembers with considerable pride his father's trust in him when he left the little town of Agira in Sicily to go to school in Catania, 70 kilometres away. "It was so far away it was like going to the United States. In those days you were assigned to a boarding house whose owner would take control of you, telling you what time to come back, what time to go out, and writing a note to the teacher if you didn't go to the school. But my father spoke to the owner of the house and said: 'My son is mature, he's free, he does not need any control. Give him the keys, he does what he wants.'

"My father also went to the teacher of the school and said: 'My son is mature, he will make his own decisions on what he is to do.' This was unique. No one else had the same degree of freedom. It gave me a great sense of responsibility. So I think in my youth I learnt how to be responsible, to take pride in what I was doing. I felt even more committed to what I was doing.

"My family was very, very warm. My father was a man of strong integrity. Simple, with not much money, but enough to allow us to study. It was a home environment with very strong values of love and integrity.

"Neither my father nor I had any idea what I would do when I was grown up. But I was good at mathematics and physics, so I decided to do engineering. Since there was not yet a faculty of engineering in Catania, I decided to go to Turin which had the best faculty for engineering at the Politecnico di Torino."

In Turin, the distance between his lodgings and the university was five kilometres. "I used to walk it every day to save the cost of the tram – 15 lira – but it was an important amount of money. I was living on a modest allowance, which my father sent me. I knew this was the maximum which he could send.

"So, during my university days, I tried to add to my allowance by sporadic teaching, for students who needed to catch up, or schools that had a teacher off sick.

"While I was an excellent student at Catania, I was not an excellent student in Turin. Not because the work was difficult, but because I didn't spend enough time studying. So instead of graduating in five years, which is the minimum time to graduate, I graduated in seven years. I was trying to combine school and life and teaching – so I took two more years than I should have done."

One of the most important lessons he learned at university was the value of a stable, secure society. It was the time of the Italian economic miracle, in the 1950s and 1960s, when the economy was growing at eight to ten per cent a year and there was a dramatic migration from the south to the north, from the countryside to the cities, to share the prosperity of Italy's industrial cities in the north. "Turin was a city of 600,000 people when I arrived in June 1954. In 1960, it had passed 1 million. When you have, in six years, a city nearly doubling in size due to immigration of poor people from the south coming to work in Fiat, or in other big industries, you get huge dislocations. It taught me some social lessons which I have applied in my professional life.

"I have learnt from what we do at ST that it is much better to put the investments where the people are, rather than moving the people to where the jobs are. It is cheaper for the company, and much better for social cohesion and avoiding social disruption.

"When hundreds of thousands of poor people came from the south, they destroyed the beautiful environment of Turin, and had a very miserable life for themselves. With the benefit of hindsight it would have been much better if big companies like Fiat had put their factories in the south than import people from the south and pay them very little. They were living in barracks and all kinds of poor conditions. It would have been much cheaper in the long run, and better for the country, to locate the factories in the south."

Forty years later, as president of ST, Pasquale followed that lesson to the letter, locating two chip factories (an investment of some $2 billion) in Catania, and significantly supporting the educational and social infrastructure of the region. Apart from the importance of the social effects of industrial decisions, he learned two other lessons while at university. One was that: 'If you want to succeed, you need discipline. The fact that I lost two years makes it very clear that there are no free lunches." The second lesson was how to live with other people. "To save money, three of us rented a cheap apartment with no heating. In the winter temperatures went down below ten degrees. Sometimes in the mornings we had to defrost the pipes before washing.

"This was a great experience because we learnt how to live together. It is not easy – three people, saving money, buying together, pooling our money for food, cooking and cleaning. It was a kind of military experience on a totally voluntary basis which teaches you respect for the others. Some other colleagues tried the same experience but broke up. We did fight sometimes but we learnt respect for each other, we learnt to make a team, to share duties, tasks and costs."

Thirty years later, when he was putting together one of the most difficult mergers in industrial history – the merger of the French company Thomson with the Italian company SGS – it was Pasquale's team-building skills that were credited with the success of an operation which most had expected to fail. "It was a good, good experience from a social point and from a personal point. And the school was a great school – the Polytechnic of Turin was a great school. It gave me not only the academic basics but a sense of responsibility and discipline."

One thing he found in himself was a fearlessness about examinations. He doesn't regret the lost two years because he was "able to sample the student life". As to his father's attitude to the lost two years, he says, "My father was always pleased with me. He was always tolerant. He'd always say: 'Don't worry, next time will be good'. I never had any reproach from my father. I was worried because there was a law in Italy which said that if you didn't finish school in time, you had to go for military service. My father would say: 'Don't worry, it will be all right'."

Electronics did not exist as an academic subject in the mid-1950s. His course was called 'Electro-mechanical – low current section'. Although the transistor had been invented in 1947 – so opening the door to the electronics era – it was not commercially manufactured until the mid-1950s. "We studied vacuum tubes, and we studied the theory behind the transistor."

At that time, he made up his mind that the fledgling electronics industry was where he wanted to be. "It was because I realised that electronics had such huge potential for revolutionising life – radio, telecommunications, the computer – and the transistor was coming. Clearly there was great potential.

"I was always studying with the idea of becoming a designer. The more the subject was theoretical, the more I was interested; the more practical the subject, the less I was interested. I was top in mathematics and top in physics. I was in love with the equation of Maxwell. It was fascinating for me, intellectually, that this man was able to discover, simply by mathematics, electromagnetic waves – that he could predicate their existence many decades before they were physically identified. That, for me, is pure genius.

"So my interest was theoretical. My idea was that as soon as I graduated, I would become a designer in a major company. I looked at Olivetti, the most important electronics company in Italy, at Siemens and at Marelli – they were all looking for engineers. Demand was far outstripping offers. Every graduate was getting twenty requests to come for an interview. I had ten interviews and got ten offers. My intention was to accept Olivetti's offer but, quite by accident, I had known a gentleman who was the representative of the Motorola agent in Italy. He said: 'You are so extrovert you would be a good salesman.' He was looking for a salesman in Turin who would sell Motorola products.

"I told him I wanted to be a designer and did not want to be a salesman. He was trying to persuade me this would be a good match with my character, and finally he says to me: 'What is the offer from Olivetti?' and I said '120,000 lira a month,' and he said: 'I'll offer you 150,000 lira a month'.

"So in March 1963, I took a job as a salesman. I did not have a driving licence so I started going around on a bicycle. Sometimes I took the tram. This lasted for about six to eight months. Then I took my driving test and bought a third-hand car – an Opel – sometimes I had to push it.

"It was a pioneering time. Fantastic. It was the beginning of ICs [integrated circuits]."

The IC – the chip – had been invented in 1958. In 1963, all the leading makers of chips worldwide were American companies. Motorola had been one of the first companies to make transistors commercially in the mid-1950s, and was also one of the first to make commercial chips. By 1963, Motorola was one of the world's top five chip manufacturers alongside Texas Instruments and Fairchild Semiconductor. Chip technology was very much a black art, and Pasquale remembers conferring with some of his ex-university colleagues, now working at Olivetti, to keep up with the changes in technology. He certainly got no help from his boss: "My boss was a lawyer who knew nothing about electronics. He was the rep of many things as well as the Motorola line."

Another hindrance was that Pasquale was not allowed to telephone or even telex Motorola because of the expense. The only contact he was allowed with the company was by mail. "You'd send a letter and one month later you'd get the answer – it might even be a price quotation for a customer!" Nonetheless, he loved the job and can still reel off the part numbers of the early 1960s Motorola product portfolio: "The diodes – the 401 and 404, the famous germanium power transistors – the 173 and 174, the 1613 and 1711, the 2218 and 2222." He makes them sound like old friends.

"I knew all the products. The catalogue was small. But times have changed because the scope is now so vast. At that time one salesman could sell the entire product portfolio of a company. Today I don't think that is possible, because you cannot sell with the same kind of competence.

"I found that being a salesman was close to my character – being in touch with people, the dialogue, the feeling of doing business rather than being a pure designer. I was OK in this kind of job.

"Then, in October 1966, when Motorola set up its own office in Milan, they hired me from the distributor, and I became a sales-man for Motorola on the Motorola payroll. Previously I had been on the payroll of the distributor. I was 30, and I was appointed the sales manager for Italy – the only employee in the country! My boss was Dedy Saban – a very, very good man.

"My experience as a sales manager was good; I started hiring some people and building a team." In 1968, he was promoted to regional director for Motorola in Italy. He was about to be put to the test. "In 1968, the famous Les Hogan [president of Motorola's semiconductor division] left Motorola, taking many of the top managers, including Dedy Saban with him."

What precipitated the move was the resignation from Fairchild Semiconductor of two of its founding stars: Robert Noyce, the president, and Gordon Moore, the head of the Fairchild laborato-ries which had first shown how chips could be commercially manufactured. Noyce and Moore were leaving to found Intel. The owner of Fairchild Semiconductor, Sherman Fairchild, responded to these resignations by offering Hogan a salary and a chunk of stock on a scale which staggered the entire industry to move over from Motorola to be president of Fairchild. Hogan was to take most of Motorola's top management with him.

"In August 1968, I was in Phoenix [HQ of Motorola's semi-conductor division] to get acquainted with my new job as regional director. One Friday, there was a panic in Motorola. 'Hogan is leaving. Everybody is leaving.' I was offered the job of general

manager for Fairchild in Europe. There was a feeling that everyone who didn't leave Motorola would die. I was offered double
the salary plus stock options – I didn't understand what they were
– I hadn't heard of them before. Dedy said: 'I'm leaving Motorola.
Follow me.' I had one night awake in Phoenix. Should I accept –
which was tempting – or should I stay? I had just been promoted.
My duty was to hold the ground rather than abandoning it for
extra money. It felt like abandoning a ship that was in trouble. It
didn't seem correct. I decided to stay. I think, at the time, my boss
appreciated the fact that I decided to stay.

"The job at Motorola was fine. In 1970 I was promoted to marketing manager for Europe and I moved from Milan to Geneva.
1971 was one of the toughest years in my life. There was a big
crisis in the industry which started at the end of 1970. I was really
under pressure because on the 30th October 1970 my daughter
Elena was born. And she had a virus, just after she was born, and
was dying in hospital. I was in the middle of two big challenges
– one was Elena, and the other was that I had to lay off people
for the first time in my life.

"It was a tremendously tough year. However, eventually, we
came through in a very good way. Redundancies were made in a
European fashion and my daughter eventually overcame the
problem and was fine.

"In 1971, I pioneered an organisational change in the semiconductor industry. I organised the marketing in a matrix – by regions
and segments. I had four regions reporting to me: Southern
Europe, Central Europe, Northern Europe and Nordic, and I had
four segments reporting to me: computer, consumer, telecommunications and industrial. They were acting in a matrix.

"The regions had responsibility for customer coverage, and the segments had responsibility for creating pan-European strategies for that segment, promoting the right products, and covering the transregional accounts. It was the first time that the matrix organisation, reflecting the importance of product segments across European countries, was put in place in Europe and, maybe, even in the United States.

"This concept of the matrix approach has since been used in many parts of my business responsibilities. It was clear that the applications dimension was becoming more important than the regional dimension. For instance, the computer needs of Olivetti in Italy, Bull in France, Nixdorf in Germany or ICL in the UK – which were our major customers at the time – were broadly similar. They had similar application requirements – they were all doing small computers, they all needed the same kind of products, so, if you wanted to maximise the return on your products, you needed the same approach to product development.

"You cannot develop a different product for Olivetti in Italy for the same application as you've developed for Nixdorf in Germany. So you need pan-European coordination in order to make sure you maximise the return on your portfolio."

By this time he was ensconced mid-way up the Motorola management structure and learning to survive in the US industrial culture as he climbed the corporate ladder. How did he cope with the politics? "I hate politics," he responds with fervour. "In Motorola, as in any corporation, there were some politics but not too many. In ST today there are not too many politics – you always have some – but it is not an environment where politics prosper. I don't like politics. I was doing my job and it was the results that counted. You can see that is the case because I was chosen as the marketing manager for Europe when I was the youngest regional manger for one of the smallest regions – Italy. There were people more senior than me who had bigger regional responsibilities. That I was made marketing manager for Europe came as a big surprise to everybody."

Were people jealous? "Jealous is not the word. People were surprised. Many of them had a legitimate aspiration to get the job, but my appointment was based on track record."

The man who appointed him to the job was Bob Heikes. "I've learnt a lot from all my bosses. Bob was one of the greatest strategists I ever met, and a visionary. I learned the importance of delegating from him, and how to match your dream to practical problems. Bob was an excellent boss and he probably had the greatest influence on me. Many people who worked for Bob did well later on in their careers.

"In the States I always respected Tom Connors – he was never my direct boss, he was always a little bit higher – but I was always very close to Tom. Eventually, when I became the international general manager in the US, John Welty was my boss and I also respected him a lot.

"All my experiences with my bosses in Motorola were good. My first boss was Dedy Saban – he was a hard task-master, very aggressive and yet very friendly. He taught me to be determined, to be persistent, to be hard-working. Dedy went to Fairchild and, many years later when I was general manager, I hired him back. So I worked for Dedy and he worked for me. We had tremendous respect for each other. As both a boss and a subordinate, our rapport was always outstanding.

"Then when I was regional manager for Italy between 1968 and 1970, my boss was Jim Finke, the marketing manager for Europe. Again, he was a great boss. He was a great strategist, liked Europe very much, he was very sensitive to the cultural differences in Europe and the richness of the culture, he was very well educated. He taught me the importance of cultural values, how to maximise these differences and how to cope with the American culture."

Did the American company culture come as a shock? Pasquale looks surprised at the question. "For me? No. I fit very well in the American culture, I found it very easy, and I think my American colleagues found me very easy. I'm a very basic person, and I think Americans are basic people and like basic people – they think that if you are performing, you are a good man; that if you are not performing, you are no good. I am the same. So I think it was an easy fit."

Does he really see himself as basic? "I'm a little bit more than basic," laughs Pasquale, "but I think the basics are very important. I think values like honouring what you commit to do, not changing your mind, being at ease with yourself, having business integrity in the broad sense are essential. I value these things in the American culture, and they are values which I have adopted myself all my life.

"My 17 years at Motorola were very good. They taught me a lot. I learnt to be a manager coping with the human side of the Italian environment and the European environment, while also coping with the American rigour of business practicality. And this, in the end, is my managerial style – marrying American rigour with a good sensibility for people.

"I believe the formative influences of my childhood, working for my father, prepared me for the American culture. My father taught me to be an optimist, to be at peace with my conscience, that if you are doing what is necessary you should not worry, to have integrity, to be very straight – this works for life, but it also works for business.

"I have tried to replicate my father's values in my own family. My family was very simple but duties were clear. In today's families they are not so clear. In my family, when I was a boy, my duties were clear. My father was the guarantee that we were safe. He was the force, the solidity, the safety. My mother was love. That's all. Very simple. We had all the love, all the care, all the attention from my mother, and all the safety, tranquillity and solidity from my father. Nothing could happen. My father would take care of us. And nothing would affect our mother's love for us. It was a very nice combination. A normal, simple, traditional family but with values built in very strongly.

"I have tried to replicate this in my own family. It is difficult because I travel a lot, but I believe my children have always felt secure, because I represented security – moral, physical and material – and my wife takes care of them, creating all the love. So I don't think they've missed the warmth of a family.

"It's a nice, old-style family which I hope will not be lost in future. There is a trend to more and more disaggregation within the family. People are getting too immersed in work and have less and less time for the family. The feeling of union which there was in families in the previous generation is not the same. This was a big contributor to a stable society. The best school is your family. No one can teach you moral values like your family can."

In the mid 1970s Pasquale's career at Motorola began to take off. He moved up another rung on the corporate ladder in 1974 with his appointment as general manager for Europe. Then, in 1977, he was made world director of marketing and a corporate vice-president. He was the first non-American corporate vice-president to be elected by the Motorola board. The job was located in Phoenix. He was later to say that his time there was the happiest of his life. In 1978 he became international general manager of the semiconductor division – responsible for one-third of the division's revenues which represented some $400 million in 1980.

Then came his great gamble. "In 1980, I was invited to run SGS. SGS was an Italian company which was desperately sick from a financial point of view. SGS had sales of around $100 million [Motorola's chip sales were then $1 billion]. SGS had been losing money for ten years. Italy was a very difficult place, with terrorism and union power making life very difficult, but I accepted the challenge and took the job."

Why? "Four reasons: first, being general manager of a division is important but it's different to being the CEO of a company. As CEO you can take full responsibility. You really can be reponsible for failure or success. Maybe if I'd waited a few years more I could have become the same in Motorola. But I thought this was important. It was a professional challenge.

"The second thing was because this was in Italy. To take up a very sick Italian company, and feel that I could turn it around, gave me a sense of national pride. So there was not only professional pride, but pride in my country.

"The third thing was homesickness. My parents were becoming older, my wife's parents were getting older, we thought it was a good time to go home; fourth, SGS had some important niche technologies like Smartpower – intelligent power. I knew because they were my competitors.

"I left Motorola in a very friendly way. I didn't leave Motorola – I went to SGS. I remember having breakfast with John Welty one morning, and at the end of the discussion he said, 'So you're leaving Motorola to join SGS?'

'Yes, John.'

'Is SGS a good company, is it in great shape?'

'No John, they are losing their shirt. They are really in difficulties.'

'I see. Well, is Italy a very nice environment to work in?'

'No John, terrorists are killing one executive a week, and the unions are really dominating the scene.'

'Are they paying you more?'

'No, John, they are paying me much less.'

'Pasquale, are you crazy?'

'Yes, John, I'm crazy'."

"I remember telling colleagues I was leaving to go to SGS. They asked me: 'What business are they in?'

'SGS is a competitor,' I replied.

'Oh really?' they said."

History was to add irony to those conversations. In 1980, Motorola's chip sales were $1 billion a year while SGS's revenues were $100 million. Twenty years later, STMicroelectronics, the renamed SGS, had chip sales worth $8 billion, level-pegging with Motorola's chip sales. ST had grown at twice the rate of Motorola between 1980 and 2000. *Now* Motorola knows that ST is a competitor.

In 1980 Pasquale went back to Italy to a difficult life – both at work and at home. "My personal life was tough because the environment was very difficult. Unions dominated the scene – it was very difficult or impossible to fire people if you wanted to restructure. Terrorism was killing one executive a week. My salary was much lower – my family discovered that life in Milan was more expensive than in Phoenix, and my salary was half what it had been. This put a strain on family life from a financial point of view. So we had some difficulties coming back home. I think this hardened my determination to succeed.

"My wife took care of the family while I took care of SGS. To begin the turnaround of the company, I immediately put three goals to the people at SGS: first we must become profitable – a business enterprise doesn't serve any purpose if it loses money. We can't say we are strategic because we make semiconductors – that is nonsense – we must make money. That was a big, big invention."

It was a 'big invention' because the chip-making operations in Europe at that time – Philips, Siemens, Thomson, Ferranti, Plessey and SGS – all had, effectively a licence to lose money from their parent companies. European governments were in the habit of subsidising chip companies on the grounds that they were a 'strategic' investment – necessary to maintain vital technologies in Europe – irrespective of whether they could make any profits from them. More often than not, European chip companies made losses. "It was normal," says Pasquale, "that semiconductor companies in Europe lost money." SGS had made losses for eleven successive years when he took over.

The second goal which Pasquale put to the SGS management was: "we must win American customer confidence. Until we can sell on a good scale in the US, we will not know if our products are any good. The endorsement of the American market will tell us if we are making the right products." At the time he took over, only ten per cent of SGS's sales – worth about $10 million – were to the US.

The third goal which he set his company was: "we are too small. We must become a member of the billion dollar club because, with $100 million, you cannot compete on the dimension of scale.

"I think most people were enthusiastic about this challenge. Many people bet on this with an enthusiasm and a dedication which is unusual A few of them didn't believe it so they quit."

Pasquale's bald account omits the most important ingredient – his personality. He is the sort of person who, if he believes in something, radiates that belief. It is almost impossible not to get caught up in his enthusiasm. His ebullience is an infectious, invigorating force. His rallying cry in those early days was: "If we don't believe it can be done, it won't be done." He made people think it could be done. Now, as one of those perpetual motion executives forever flying around ST locations, he is still the company's chief motivator. He encourages his people's creativity, backs innovative projects and pushes them to achieve, always contributing his enthusiasm and commitment.

He accepts no limitations on what is achievable either by ST or by Europe. He can be explosive when it is suggested that Europe is incapable of competing with Asia and America. That his people know that there is no one more personally committed to the success of ST than the boss, is a powerful energising force for the whole company. It took him three years to cajole, plan, inspire and fight to get SGS into profit. "We became profitable for the first time in June 1983. I believe this was the first time that a European company became profitable in that period. Because the other European companies were suffering from the same problems as SGS – a difficult competitive environment, and an inability to penetrate the American market – we showed them that semiconductors could be viable in Europe.

"But then, of course, we were still very small. I was convinced that we needed to take a major step to reach economies of scale. I started looking in Europe for contacts. Thomson Semiconductor was a company with the right characteristics for us for joining forces. So in 1986 we started talks.

"Jacques Noels was the boss of Thomson Semiconducteurs. Jacques and I had known each other for many years, since he was in TI (Texas Instruments) and I was in Motorola. So we started bottom-up discussions. We thought it would be good to merge. Then we asked our shareholders – they were very courageous in view of the difficulties of merging two heavily unionised companies, which meant it would be difficult to rationalise and restructure, and which were controlled by different governments." Both SGS and Thomson were wholly-owned subsidiaries of government-owned bodies.

"There could only be one CEO and they chose me, very likely because SGS had already started to change, and was already profitable, and had shown that it could be done. Jacques was extremely supportive and said: 'Whatever I can do in the transition I will do.' That's how ST was formed and I began my greatest professional adventure.

"We carried out a merger that seemed impossible. Two companies that were, in different ways, both sick. There was Thomson which had heavy losses, but no debt, because it was a division of a group, and there was SGS, which was marginally profitable, but which had dramatic debts.

"The combined company in 1987 had sales of $850 million, were losing $200 million, and had debts of $650 million. So everyone was betting that within a couple of years, or sooner, we would go broke."

What happened in the next seven years was totally astonishing. In 1994, Pasquale was telling an industry conference: "Seven years ago the only thing people said was: 'The European semiconductor industry is dead – it should be left to the Japanese and the Americans.' Now we are saying: 'How do we keep this success going?' "

ST had grown at an average 17.6 per cent a year since 1987. Its 1994 sales topped $2.6 billion and showed a profit of $362 million, its debt was virtually zero, and over $1 billion was invested that year in R&D and new manufacturing capacity. It was a fantastic turnaround. How was it done? "After the merger in 1987, we focused on the pluses. There were tremendous synergies and possibility of savings. We closed four or five plants in three years. We rationalised manufacturing, transferring processes from one plant to the other. We unified the administration costs, saving a lot of money.

"There was strong complementarity in the product portfolio. There were technologies in which one company was the leader like the Smartpower of SGS and the BiCMOS of Thomson. The geographical match was good – SGS was stronger in Asia where we had wafer manufacturing while Thomson was stronger in the US because of its purchase of Mostek in Dallas. So we were very complementary and had good savings possibilities. The magic was how we managed to integrate the two teams. It was an outstanding integration." The team-building and social skills, nurtured thirty years before in a freezing apartment in Turin, now came into play. His fluency in the major European languages played a part. But, mainly, it was the sheer force of his personality that accomplished a creative merging of strengths, when the most likely outcome would have seemed a bloody and destructive political fight.

"We eventually accomplished the merger much, much faster than anyone would have thought possible. In 1988, the first full year of combined operation, we were profitable at the operating level. In other words, the loss was only due to restructuring costs. In 1989 we were bottom-line profitable – a very small profit – but we had a black bottom line."

It was something the company was to maintain and improve. In 1996, the company not only had a gross profit margin of over 40 per cent, but it also entered the ranks of the world's top ten chip companies with sales of $4 billion. In the recession years of 1997 and 1998, ST kept investing in R&D and manufacturing and was in good shape for the 1999 upturn. By then Pasquale was raising the bar again and setting the company's sights on becoming one of the world's top five chip companies. Everything he's said he'll achieve, he has achieved. Growth of over 50 per cent in 2000 suggests that ST is on track for a top five ranking. He certainly believes it himself. "If you are a long-time executive in the semiconductor industry you need a lot of faith – and I have it."

His faith in the semiconductor industry has been accompanied, in recent years, by a belief in conservation. In the late 1980s, when he had been president of ST for some years, his children, Carmelo, Elena and Vittorio – but principally the eldest, Carmelo – challenged him as to whether his values extended to accepting other obligations than simply those to his shareholders. With the manufacturing industry apparently destroying the environment, Carmelo worked away at his father's conscience, eventually persuading him of the importance of environmentally friendly strategies in business.

Now Pasquale has all the fervour of a convert, committing ST to conservation measures which far outstrip any obligation required by local or national law. While many businessmen pay lip service to environmental issues, Pasquale publishes detailed, quantifiable environmental targets for ST, and monitors how successfully they are being achieved. For instance, he has committed, and is on track, to reduce carbon dioxide emissions from 500 tons to 80 tons per annum between 1990 and 2010; he has reduced the use of paper by the company from 240 tons to 55 tons per annum in the last three years; he has committed ST to be using renewable energy source for 5 per cent of its total energy requirement by 2010. There is a whole string of similar, measurable commitments.

In following this path, he has found some side benefits. First, ST's environmental stance is attractive to highest-quality employees, and in the intellect-driven chip business, high-quality people give a company competitive edge. Second, environmentally friendly technologies have, in many cases, turned out to be more industrially efficient and more profitable. Third, by going further than current regulations require, ST is getting ahead of its competitors in practising disciplines which other companies will, eventually, be legally obliged to adopt. This gives ST a future competitive advantage.

ST has won many awards for quality and conservation, the most prestigious of which are the US Climate Protection Award and America's top award for industrial quality, the Malcolm Baldridge Quality Award. ST has also won the European Quality Award.

Pasquale has received two knighthoods – one from the Italian government, the order *Cavaliere del Lavoro* and one from the French government – the *Chevalier de la Legion d'Honneur*.

For a while, it seemed, no one but him believed that Europe could compete in the chip industry on equal terms with America and Asia. Now, this is happening.

ULRICH SCHUMACHER

Propelled into stardom as president of Siemens' billion-dollar chip business at the age of 37, Ulrich Schumacher immediately hit disaster as the chip industry went into the longest and deepest slump in its history. After losing $700 million in 1998, he steered the company into independence from Siemens, renaming it Infineon Technologies, and taking it public in 2000 with a valuation which made it one of Germany's ten most valuable companies.

B orn into a family which owned an engineering business making electrical transformers in Cologne, Schumacher's choice of career was not surprising. What was surprising was that, at 27, armed with a doctorate in electrical engineering, he joined one of Germany's staidest companies – the 150 year-old Siemens.

"The idea was that I would come back and run the family company with my brother, but I decided to go and work for a major company first. My father is a very strong character, and my brother gets along with him better than I do, and I thought I'd go into big industry then come back, not as my father's son but as an equal."

So why Siemens?

"My father's company was a middle-sized company, very entrepreneurial and performance-oriented. So I looked for something opposite to that – to what at that time was perceived to be a slow-moving giant – and that brought me to Siemens."

Ever since, he has been prising open the steely walls of German propriety to propel the company into the freebooting, risk-taking culture of the international high-tech industry. He likes to challenge received wisdom, confront convention and play the maverick.

He was lucky in his timing. Siemens was going through a period in which it was gradually realising that it had to be more of an international company. It had to have more of an Anglo-Saxon flavour to its culture and Schumacher – open-minded, entrepreneurial and willing to take a risk – was just the man to encourage it.

Personally, he's very engaging, tall – 6 foot 5 inches – and with a disarming smile. He could charm a bird off a tree, which probably accounts for his reputation within Siemens as a shrewd practitioner of company politics. In contrast with his conventional background, Schumacher is a bit of a rebel. Within such a traditional company as Siemens, he's been seen as a free-thinking iconoclast but, although he has upset many people by being outspoken, he has prospered. And the reason why is because he is clearly playing for results, not effect. For instance, when he joined Siemens' semiconductor division – a happy choice made by Siemens – his first job was to look at the chip testing equipment. He found that, with chip sales revenues of only DM 1 billion, the company was spending DM 60 million a year on test equipment. 'They bought the fastest, best, most expensive – not the most appropriate. Cost of ownership was my issue from Day 1."

He realised that radical change was needed but encountered huge, entrenched resistance to it. "The more resistance I meet, the more motivated I am. I don't know why; it's part of my character. If things run smoothly, with no challenge, things get boring very, very fast. In business, as in private life, the more you have to struggle, the more alive you feel.

"There were many, many challenges in Siemens. The good thing was this huge potential in the company – there were many very bright people at the working level, many of them frustrated and demotivated. And there was huge resistance to change at management levels."

In two and a half years dealing with the test equipment area, he cut the annual spend on equipment to under $20 million while increasing productivity by 40 per cent. He was then appointed to the staff of Jurgen Knorr, who was president of Siemens Semi-conductors from 1983 to 1996.

"I need a new challenge every three years. I divide my life into periods of three years. I always think: 'What is a reasonable time to try something new?' I think that you can't have a major impact in less than two years and, if you haven't made an impact after three years, then it's not reasonable to think that you can make an impact after that. For three years I commit myself to whatever I've started, and take on all the challenges and struggles. Then I like a new challenge. Siemens has always managed to provide a challenge – it will never become boring.

"I had two and a half years in this equipment job, I was about three with Mr Knorr. Then I joined DRAM marketing and later business management for three years. I created the Standard Division and, in 1996, I took over Siemens Semiconductors and then there was the challenge of the IPO [Initial Public Offering]. So it was always something new."

It had been his original intention to go back to Cologne and to his father's transformer business after a couple of years at Siemens. But Siemens kept him interested and engaged by giving him new challenges. "After five years there was no way back." And no way out, it seemed – a German car manufacturer offered him several times his salary to leave Siemens, but by then he was hooked on the job and stayed put. After two and half years on Knorr's staff, he was offered the job of marketing either telecommunications chips or DRAM [Dynamic Random Access Memory] chips. Telecoms chips were a stable and prosperous area. DRAMs were in a mess. He chose DRAMs. Why? "I had already been through a couple of cycles of taking a challenging job, doing what needed to be done, making many enemies and having a big success so that no one could kill you. I knew that my method of working means you have to have a job which allows you, in a reasonable timeframe, to show success. Otherwise you're dead.

"Nothing was running properly in DRAMs. As an assistant to Mr Knorr I studied and worked on DRAM basically 50 per cent of my time. Everything was wrong – development, sales, productivity, fabs [an abbreviation for 'wafer fabrication units'] – everything was wrong. On the other hand we had a really good telecommunications business – very good products, very stable.

"I assumed that I could achieve much more in a much shorter time in DRAM marketing than in telecoms chip marketing. In telecoms, whatever kind of new products you create or design, or influence, the earliest time you can see them in production is three years later, and making an impact in the market takes another two years. So the earliest you can see results is five years. And in five years, the politicians will have killed you – five times."

Why was he so certain that the 'politicians' within Siemens were out to kill him?

"Everybody talks about a new management culture but people always just look at it in a unilateral way. The culture that you can criticise your boss, that you can have different opinions, that you are loyal to your company and not to your boss – which is a completely different thing – is not the way to make friends.

"In an extremely performance-oriented organisation, you love to have this kind of person; in a more stable organisation, you like to kill this kind of person – they are simply disturbing factors.

"I was accepted by a few people who thought the same way as I did, and resistance from many established people – especially managers – who saw me as a threat because I always wanted to do things differently to how they had been done in the past."

An example was the OEM DRAM business. 'I wanted to do an OEM [i.e. subcontract] business with DRAMs so that I could direct my own production onto key accounts. The management didn't want to OEM the DRAM business. They saw the idea as a threat. It took me nine months to get approval by claiming that I was going to do it with the Japanese who are our friends. Two months later I was doing 90 per cent of my business with the Koreans. So there was always a struggle to find a path through the organisation.

"So I was always considered somehow as a threat. I have not changed much. Whenever you do something different you're considered a threat. Ninety per cent of people hate change; change gives them a feeling of uncertainty, of losing things. But in this industry you are a change agent. Half the job is looking at ways to do things better. But very few people supported me in doing that. For instance, when I was in DRAM marketing, the perception of my boss was that marketing was some kind of in-house sales route to bring the product to the customer. I had only a six week marketing course and I said: 'No, marketing is about redirecting all the resources of the company towards the market.' Which is a completely different concept. What I wanted to do was to decide on the products, to define cost targets, timeframes. My boss just

wanted me to take products out of inventory and find a customer
for them, which is a completely different job. So there was a
disconnect. And I was fighting with my development people
because, at that time, we had a 72 square millimetre one megabit
DRAM and I knew that Micron's [Micron Technology of Idaho – a
rival DRAM producer] one megabit DRAM was significantly smaller. I learnt that from the literature, and we also did some reverse
engineering, but nobody wanted to hear that."

So Schumacher chose one person from all the main departments involved in DRAM and flew them over to Idaho to visit
Micron. They found that Micron's chip was 45 square millimetres
which meant it was some 30 per cent cheaper to manufacture
than Siemens' DRAM, making Siemens' product uncompetitive in
the market. "I think Micron felt sorry for us. They were working
on a 17 square millimetre cut-down one meg. For two days they
showed us everything. They showed us through the production
lines. It was lucky they didn't throw us out. I really think it was
because they felt so sorry for these poor little guys that they said:
'Let's show them the real world and then they'll give up'.

"After we came back from Idaho, there was no more discussion
about what we had to do. It was a result of shock. Without it, it
would have been impossible to make these people move. The
knowledge was there, it was simply that the people were not willing to take the risk, they were waiting for someone else to make
a move, asking: 'Should we do a design shrink or should we do
a process shrink?' After that, it wasn't a question of my pushing
these people to make a shrink, but slowing them down. Their
targets were becoming so aggressive they were frightening me.

"Everything was like that – a struggle. For instance, we had one customer in Switzerland who ordered $10 million worth of DRAM a year and the cost of that sale was 15 per cent. He ordered four times a year. So it cost $1.5 million to take these four orders a year. But we couldn't argue. Not at all. So we said: 'We can't afford to deliver any more.' And after two months, we started negotiations again and agreed a 6 per cent sales cost, which was still expensive but a lot better than 15 per cent.

"With this background, when we approached the next country organisation they had already been warned what to expect and it was a little easier, and they came back and said to us, 'OK. OK.'

"In twelve months, I reduced sales and marketing costs by DM 90 million. When I took over DRAM marketing, we had DM 400 million of revenues, and heavy losses. I took DM 90 million out of sales and marketing and gained another DM 80 million out of price increases. So I had a DM 170 million impact out of my three-person department in twelve months. This was something which no one could say anything against."

Then he had a product struggle. "I had a customer where I was the sole source and my customer gave me 18 months' notice that he needed a 4 megabit by 16 DRAM [DRAMs come in widths – by 1, by 4, by 8, or by 16] for his printer. I went to my development department and said: 'I need a 4 megabit by 16.' They said: 'Wait. We'll develop a 4 megabit by 8, and after that we'll develop a 4 megabit by 16.' I said: 'I have no customers for a 4 megabit by 8. None of my customers wants a 4 megabit by 8 – the only company who wanted a 4 by 8 was Apple – but I have many customers who would use a 4 megabit by 16.' So I went to the business division manager who said: 'We will follow the recommendation of the development department and develop a 4 megabit by 8'. Well, after we'd developed the 4 megabit by 8, Apple slowed down and I lost my customer for the 4 megabit by 16, so the damage was absolutely huge. At this time I felt my impact in the company had become limited. Shortly after that I was given my boss's job.

"It was the same story with manufacturing. Manufacturing was completely independent. If it had idle capacity at the end of the year, they took all my wonderful chips and put them into DIP packages – but I had no customers for DIP packages; all my customers wanted SOJ packages. But they just wanted to fulfil their manufacturing performance targets. So I ended up the year with huge inventory on DIPs where I had no customers. Siemens was a tremendous place to fight. It was a lot of fun at this time.

"We had a joke that we were a three-man marketing department who basically integrated the rest of Infineon over the years into this three-person organisation. First we took development, then we took the fabs, then the ChipCard (Smartcard division), then microcontrollers and then we took the rest."

Throughout this period, the DRAM business was fighting against closure. Because of the way costs were allocated at Siemens, DRAM appeared to be the heaviest loss-making product because most of the costs of developing new technology were charged to the DRAM product sector. As the sector which was the first to use the most advanced process technology as it came out of the laboratories, that was natural. But it meant that the financial figures for the other product sectors looked better than they should, because they got the same technology essentially for nothing – as a hand-me-down from the DRAM sector. Of course, if the DRAM sector had folded, the costs would have had to fall on another product sector which then, too, would very likely have fallen into loss. Nonetheless, there was pressure from almost everyone to close the DRAM business, from the Siemens board to the people in Siemens' semiconductor division. "Everybody except Mr Knorr wanted to close the DRAM business – he was the only guy who believed in it.

"Those years in DRAM – 1991–1994 – were the most satisfying years of my business life so far: because everyone thought the DRAM business was dead, there was a decision to close it and no one wanted to be associated with it, so I had the ultimate freedom. No one could really interfere, because no one wanted to be seen with a failure."

Then, in 1995, everything changed. "In 1995, the DRAM business made a profit of DM 600 million on sales of DM 1.7 billion.

"I will never forget the day when a board member called me and said: 'Mr Schumacher, your business is so big, you can't take care of it by yourself. I'm going to help you.' I politely rejected the offer. But things were changing. Mr Knorr was getting close to retiring. I guess I had a few supporters on the top level of Siemens who voted for me as CEO of the semiconductor group (in 1996). The good news was that now I could really influence the whole group. The bad news was that the market was running into the most disastrous period it had ever seen."

The DRAM market turned in 1996. DRAM prices, which had been $50 per chip at the start of the year, were $12 by the end. Producers, stuffed with windfall profits from the early 1990s, had invested in new production capacity which guaranteed a lengthy downturn as a flooded market kept depressing prices further and further. In three years a market which had been worth $40 billion a year dropped to $14 billion, with producers losing a collective $10 billion in 1998.

Suddenly, from Golden Boy he was Whipping Boy, as the money-eating chip factories churned out tens of millions of chips, each of which added to the company's losses. He still managed to record a small profit in 1997 – $65 million on sales of $3.5 billion – but the following year the full horror of the story became apparent with a recorded loss of $723 million. Compounding the problem had been the collapse of several Asian economies (the so-called 'Asian Contagion') which led to the International Monetary Fund (IMF) being called in to bail them out. The situation could not have been worse for a company which had gambled heavily on the increasing market share by investing in new capacity.

In the gloom of 1998, Schumacher had to acknowledge: "The Asian crisis is not over – no one knows what's happening in China. We have to admit that we don't believe there'll be a tremendous revival in the market any time soon. It's always been a strange industry, but somehow you could cope with its behaviour. But historically there's never been a time when the market shrank ten per cent (1996), grew four per cent (1997) and then shrank twelve per cent (1998) I don't know what will happen next year but I'm pessimistic about whether we'll see growth."

Typically, he went on the attack, shooting from the hip at all those he saw as responsible for the problem: the European Union (EU), the International Monetary Fund and the Korean government. At the time, he complained: "We tried to get the EU to take action against dumping but we were not successful. The EU doesn't realise what the Koreans are doing to prices. I'm very disappointed by the actions of the EU – they said they'd take quick action if there was evidence of dumping but the EU now says that to take action against the Koreans would be discriminatory, because everyone is dumping.

"Siemens is a responsible company, 150 years old, which finances growth out of its earnings, but the Koreans have started a war with debt financing. They are still pushing prices down and still investing in capacity to buy market share. Not even the oil producing countries behaved in such an idiotic way. I blame the Koreans, and the Koreans, in my view, are backed by the IMF. I cannot compete with the financial strength of the IMF."

The Koreans responded furiously. "IMF funds are used exclusively to repay foreign debts and increase the foreign currency reserves of the Bank of Korea and not bail out or subsidise private industries," responded Hye-Bum Choi of the Korean Semiconductor Industry Association. The Korean government complained about Schumacher's remarks to the German Ministry of Foreign Affairs. It didn't worry him. He still kept blaming the Koreans, the IMF and the EU. Asked how he personally coped with the reality of a collapsed market and huge losses, he replies: "We rely much more on whether we are satisfied with us than what the external world thinks. The external world will never give you the acceptance and credit you want. That's something my father taught me from my early days. If your model in life does not depend on feedback from your environment, then you do not get demotivated by outside events.

"The demotivating thing was that the market didn't pick up. But pressure from the outside was probably something that was motivating us even more. We really wanted to show the world what we could do."

Through the dog days Schumacher maintained one important institution – every night he and his top managers would go out for dinner. "We spent every single night at this little Italian restaurant near our offices. We got there between nine and ten and we were there till it closed at one in the morning. We were always the last people there. They always had to throw us out. It was extremely important for the team, after the pressure and stress of the day, to come alive again. Physically it was exhausting but psychologically it was absolutely mandatory. To go home with all the pressure and frustration is not good. We didn't miss a single day. We had some problems with our wives."

How did he cope with that? "I wouldn't say I coped with it. I found a way to make it feasible, but it was far from being ideal."

The dinners were, he says: "an important element of our culture." They were was also important for his own survival: "Having the team behind me, on at least two occasions, allowed me to survive. For political reasons a company might be willing to fire a CEO, but it's very difficult to fire a whole board – it doesn't look good. In the early days, my only protection was the team."

With the collapse of the DRAM market, the team had to look elsewhere for profitable revenues. They were extremely difficult to find. 'We had a good RF [radio frequency] business and a good business in power discretes – everything else was a disaster." They prepared a 'logic attack' which, by 2000, had resulted in logic products accounting for 60 per cent of Infineon's revenues. But, in 1998, the business was still haemorrhaging money. Deprived of EU protection from dumping, and battered by the effects of Korea's IMF money, Schumacher was forced into making what he called the toughest decision of his career – the closure of a UK chip factory which had only recently been opened by the Queen. It was a measure of his persuasiveness inside Siemens that he could get the board's approval for the closure. The UK factory had been fought for at the highest levels, with British Prime Minister John Major personally lobbying the president of Siemens, Heinrich von Pierer.

The plant was losing £150 million a year, accounting for 30 per cent of the 1998 losses. "I am sorry that the people in Tyneside are paying the bill," he said at the time. "It is awful that we have to close a factory. I hated the decision – it was one of the toughest points in my business life so far. The question is whether you have people unemployed in Korea or in Europe."

To his credit, Schumacher did not leave the closure to local management. He went to Tyneside and told the employees there personally, then flew to London to explain it to the media. He refused to attribute the closure to the strong pound which would have been an easy get-out, instead putting the blame on market conditions, the EU, the IMF and the Koreans. It was an awful day and the pain was showing by the end.

Three months later, in November 1998, he was thinking and talking very positively, having been told by von Pierer that he was to be spun off as a separate company. It was a good time for von Pierer to do it. Financial analysts have never liked semiconductor companies, seeing them as hungry consumers of capital for wildly fluctuating returns. With the results from the parent Siemens company looking weak, and the semiconductor division losing DM 1 billion in a year, telling the markets that the semiconductor division was going to be divested was a way to minimise the hit his share price might have taken. "The losses were the door opener to the IPO," says Schumacher.

The news galvanised Schumacher into activity. He told a press conference, "the timing is excellent. For three years I've been planning for this. The only way from here is up. The only question is, how fast?"

It was a virtuoso performance for someone who'd just lost DM 1 billion, whose market was flat on its back, and whose industrial sector was very poorly rated by the stock markets. He assured employees that "all the sites are safe." He committed himself to maintaining the R&D. Many noted that he'd shed some 50 lb in weight in the preceding three months.

Siemens delayed the IPO for eighteen months, until the spring of 2000, when a recovery in the chip business was underway, and when stock market sentiment was in favour of technology stocks. In the meantime, Schumacher moved quickly to make the Siemens semiconductor division a separate company. The name Infineon was chosen – very much in line with the modern trend of suggesting desirable qualities, like Lucent (formerly AT&T Technologies) as in shining, or Agilent (formerly Hewlett-Packard) as in flexible, fast moving, agile. Infineon suggested infinite possibilities.

His knuckles got rapped again, by America's Securities and Exchange Commission (SEC). Shortly before he took the company public on the New York Stock Exchange, he said in response to Samsung's forecast that they'd make $2 billion profit on memory chips in 1999: "Whatever they do, we should be able to do 50 per cent of that." The SEC, which has strict regulations that pre-IPO statements by management should not hype companies' expectations, took a dim view.

His knuckles suffered again when he said before the first sale of shares in Infineon: "I'd prefer a low valuation. Of course Siemens would like as high a valuation as possible because they are getting the money, but if I have a high share price from the start I'm going to be under pressure to maintain it." The Siemens board pointed out to him that he was still a member of it, and shouldn't really be saying that the company's interests were not his main concern.

Somehow one doubts whether these incidents embarrassed Schumacher. The self-confidence to speak the truth, and the strength to shrug off the flak, make him a leader to whom his engineers relate. Engineers are unimpressed by bullshit – after all, you can't lie about Ohm's Law – so having a straight-shooter as a boss is important in an engineering environment.

Ultimately the success of a high-tech company depends on its engineers. "To make these people happy is very, very important. You have to structure the company around these people. That's the big challenge at the moment. Engineers are more complex animals than you think. Money is not the only way to their hearts."

Providing them with interesting projects and the chance to see their products perform in the market is the key to maintaining their involvement, he reckons.

One of the Siemens traditions he has maintained is that of being a great engineering company. Instead of looking outside to license products, Schumacher has put his engineers to work on interesting and demanding engineering projects. For instance, Infineon designed both a microprocessor core called Tricore and a DSP core called Carmel. The latter was a particularly bold venture because the market for DSPs is dominated by the US company Texas Instruments (TI). Asked why he went for such an expensive and risky strategy, Schumacher replied simply: "Why should we leave the market to TI?"

One of his strongest drives is to show that the Americans do not have a God-given right to chip markets. He believes Europe can succeed in them, and wants to demonstrate it. As well as processor cores, he set teams of engineers onto two of the hottest areas in the chip market. One is chips for mobile telephones; the other is chips which beef up ordinary phone lines to increase performance to allow, for instance, pictures and even video to be sent along them. The greatest of his engineering commitments was to take the global leadership role in a $1 billion project to pioneer the chip industry's shift from using eight inch wafers to twelve inch wafers. Schumacher persuaded the German federal government to invest in the programme, and formed a partnership with Motorola to pursue the project in Dresden. The project has led the chip industry into a new process era, giving Infineon a good manufacturing technology base for the future.

He knows that he also has to promote a reward-related culture. One of his main preoccupations has been to find a way around the legal barriers, spread equity among all the employees, and create a performance-orientated compensation culture. So, like many before him in the chip business, he had to inculcate a company culture which will encourage success within a national culture which is unsympathetic to it. Andrew Rickman talks about tackling exactly the same problem when he started up Bookham Technology in the UK and, many years before him, Gordon Moore faced it when establishing Fairchild Semiconductor in Silicon Valley itself.

Whereas many bosses like to enter meetings last, making an entrance when everyone else has arrived, you can enter a conference room to find him sitting there by himself waiting for everyone else. It may seem trivial, but it's indicative of a man who's not playing for show, but to win.

In 1998, he was elected a main board director – the youngest person ever to have been elected to the Siemens board. He was 39 years old.

He appears to relish the chip industry, comparing it to his favourite sport of motor racing, as: "Fast, risky, and expensive – but highly rewarding." Fancifully, he describes those engaged in it as "modern gladiators."

Colleagues remember his Monday morning attempts to beat his own speed record (2 hours 43 minutes) for the 615 kilometre drive from his home town near Cologne to Siemens' offices in Munich when returning from the weekend.

He can be very amusing. Confronted with the news that his competitor Motorola was giving away free licences for one of its processor cores and asked if he'd follow suit, he whipped back with: "Yeah, we're adopting that model for the Luxembourg market." Asked if he'd challenge Intel in the x86 business he quipped: "I've already got one business (DRAM) with the potential to ruin ourselves – I don't need two."

He sees nothing strange in making friends with, and voicing admiration for, his competitors – for instance Steve Appleton, president of arch-rival Micron Technology. He's a reformer, a questioner of established procedures, with the confrontational, speak-up-for-yourself style which the intellect-driven chip industry has developed for itself. If results are valued more highly than management egos, it is necessary for the most junior person to speak up if the boss is wrong. If management egos are the priority, then no chip company has a prayer of a chance of success.

When, in the depths of his memory chip losses, he was asked if he felt personally vulnerable, he responded: "Nobody can be invulnerable in this company – in this industry, I meant to say."

The egalitarian company culture was originated at Fairchild in the 1950s by Robert Noyce and Gordon Moore and became the model for Silicon Valley chip companies. The rationale behind the model is that, if you want everyone to take personal responsibility for the results of the projects they are working on, to internalise the company's values and goals, and to put in the often excessive time needed to succeed, then everyone has to be valued as an individual and rewarded appropriately for their contribution.

His insistence that Europe has the opportunity to be globally competitive – if it only makes the effort – resulted in his 'Wake Up, Europe' initiative which he and two other CEOs started after the 1999 Davos World Economic Forum. Deriding ineffectual European political systems, he said: "The time has come to apply benchmarking to the political scene in Europe."

In March 2000 came the long-awaited IPO as Siemens sold off 29 per cent of its shareholding in Infineon. Offered at 35 euros on the Frankfurt stock exchange, they quickly ran up to 75 euros, valuing the company at over 45 billion euros which made it Germany's seventh most valuable industrial company. The company also launched on the New York Stock Exchange. The shares hit $80 and, six months after the launch, stood at $65. It was the second-highest valued IPO of shares in German history after the IPO of Deutsche Telekom.

Sometimes it needs a free spirit to bring about necessary change. For Infineon, Siemens and the European semiconductor industry, Schumacher has been a liberating influence.

DICK SKIPWORTH

Dick Skipworth, the chairman of Memec, was brought up on a farm. An early interest in electricity led him to his first job designing electrical equipment. Attracted by the growth potential of microchips, he moved into that industry as a salesman. In 1974 he founded Memec, a distributor of high tech components. In 1991, he sold the company to the German company Veba for £75 million while staying on as chairman. In 2000, he was one of a consortium of investors that bought Memec back for $760 million. In 2000, Memec had sales of over $3 billion.

"From an early age I was the one who did the lights for the Christmas tree," says Dick. He liked to play with batteries and everything electrical as a child on a Lincolnshire farm. He was one of five children and the origins of his independence of mind may lie in the thirteen-year gap between him and his youngest sibling: "almost a different generation," he says.

There is always the feeling of a mistake with such an age gap. Dick laughs when he's asked his birthday – 4th September – implying a Christmas conception. "I was always somewhat different in the family – something to do with being a very late child – I grew up with grown-ups," he says. He was a roamer, sometimes not returning from primary school until half past seven in the evening after going off on a jaunt. "I gave Mother nightmares, she always said I'd done lots of things the others never did."

One of these was poaching trout and this brought him into conflict with his father. But he happily recalls: "I'd sneak the trout to my mother who would cook them."

Many years later, when Dick had floated a company on the London Stock Exchange making himself a multi-millionaire, his father still tried to keep him on the straight and narrow. "You're only a millionaire on paper," he'd tell Dick. But Dick is proud that: "he read all the Memec annual reports."

Dick's speech has a farmer's resonance – quiet and considered. Maybe the solitude of their life makes farmers careful and deliberate in their judgements and this is reflected in their speech. Others have also noticed this quality. "You better listen when Dick speaks because there's a gem in almost everything he says," says one of America's most successful high-tech entrepreneurs, Bernie Vonderschmitt, founding president of high-flying Silicon Valley company Xilinx.

There is also a physical resemblance to a farmer in Dick's square-cut features and ruddy complexion – though now that owes as much to the sea as to the land. Inside there must also still be something of the farmer because, when he first became rich after floating on the stock exchange, he bought a farm. He named it after the family farm which was called Severalls because it was made up of several different pieces of land. Asked why he bought it, he jokingly replies: "the call of the soil." His father's judgement on the purchase was brutal, but accurate: "Bloody silly idea, you'll lose a lot of money."

A key to Dick's success was the local grammar school. An excellent academic and sporting establishment, it had some distinguished former pupils including the poet Alfred, Lord Tennyson, and the Arctic explorer Sir John Franklin. They impressed him. "They had charisma. I had aspirations to be like them."

Aspirations but not application. "I was not a favourite with the headmaster," he says. "He said I was 'lethargic' in one of my reports. I didn't know what it meant. I was a complete failure in arts and languages and found sciences much easier."

Many years later the headmaster wrote a book. Many former pupils were mentioned in it. "Not me," laughs Dick. "There were pupils who had become civil servants and MPs, people who had artistic talents and those who went into the military – but not one single mention of a businessman."

School fostered two instincts in him: competitiveness and fear of failure. The first came from success in cross-country running and getting a place in the soccer First XI; the second from nearly being downgraded from the A stream to the B stream.

"The fright of being downgraded made me think I had better pull my socks up and start working. I came very close to the edge. Then I started becoming second, third and even top in physics – they couldn't understand it, they thought I had been cheating."

It was a pattern that was to repeat itself throughout his life. "If you could plot my career you'd see periods when it's gone up, followed by a slacking-off period, followed by a violent waking up. It's a sequence that's repeated itself four or five times."

Achievements he fondly remembers are building a one valve radio and an electric motor. A deep impression came from a visit arranged for the school cadet corps by REME (Royal Electrical and Mechanical Engineers) to the Royal Radar Establishment (RRE) at Malvern, Worcestershire where the pioneering work on radar was done which saved the country in the Battle of Britain.

He decided that he wanted to become an electrical engineer. The careers master was 'useless' – suggesting jobs in local garages and banks – but Dick found a reference in a physics book to the company British Thomson Houston (BTH) which led him to apply to them for an apprenticeship, which he got.

It was a tough life. The pay was 44 shillings and sixpence (£2.22) a week and lodgings had to be paid for out of that. He finished the course and achieved the AMIEE (Associate Member of the Institute of Electrical Engineers) qualification. He got his first job as a professional engineer at AEI (Associated Electrical Engineering – later taken over by GEC) designing amplifiers for radar.

At that time, Dick was commuting from Rugby (where he had digs and which was closer to his girlfriend) to Leicester. It was quite a long way, and one day he saw an advertisement in the local paper asking for engineers for a new R&D (research and development) centre being set up near Rugby by Associated Engineering. He got the job and worked on a project developing petrol injection systems for cars which, in 1965, was well ahead of its time.

The German company Bosch had many of the fundamental patents in the area, and the skill of the job lay in designing products which did the same job as the Bosch products, but did not infringe their patents. "Conditions were marvellous, the facilities were marvellous and I had a superb job," says Dick. In years to come he was often to look back with nostalgia, and some regret, on those days. It might have been a nice place to stay.

"We used to get frequent visits from semiconductor sales people, because a number of our research projects could have turned into products requiring very high volumes of semiconductors," he recalls. "One of them, David Kremer from Transitron [a

US semiconductor company, now defunct] took me out to lunch and said, 'We're looking for technical sales people.' Now at the time I had a 1938 Morris 8, and Kremer had a great big flashy Ford Consul, so I said: 'Do I get a car like yours?' and he said: 'Not quite like mine, but you will get a car.' I said: 'I'm interested.' So I got into the semiconductor industry for all the wrong reasons."

The change from the comfortable, protected life of an R&D engineer to the nitty gritty existence of a salesman was tough. "I didn't know what selling something meant," says Dick, "I had never been in a sales office."

The sales office in Ealing was a far cry from the peace and quiet of an R&D facility – it seemed to him a strange, alien place of ringing telephones and frantic activity. "I had hardly ever been to London before. They gave me this big yellow catalogue and told me to familiarise myself with the products."

There was no sales course or formal induction procedure. "My boss, Dennis O'Connell, said: 'Go and practice around the North Circular Road' – that was the full extent of my sales training.

"I probably made a hell of a mess of it. I thought customers would be more than eager to buy from me. I soon discovered that was not quite the case. Some of them were quite rude," he says ruefully.

The best thing about the job was the car – a Ford Zephyr – an upgrade from a Consul. "It was a horrible thing really – a great big body with no guts to it but, to me, it was like a Rolls Royce."

Otherwise, it was tough. "It was a lonely time. I didn't know anyone. I didn't know what I was doing. I didn't know where I was going." The challenge stimulated something within him. "The most difficult companies were the ones which interested me most

– like the ones which said: 'We don't see sales people.' There was always something there to crack. And you could . . . you could crack it."

Then came another major crunch in his life. "It was like the situation I remember at school. Dennis called a sales meeting one day. There were only three or four of us. He said: 'It's a bit flat, it's going down and the area going down quickest is Dick's.' After that I thought: 'Oops. I'd better start working. I'd better get stuck in.' I needed the job. I had a wife and young son to keep. I decided it was necessary to double my efforts.

"In the first six months after coming out of a cushy, protected, easy engineering job, I had often thought, why can't I get a nice job like I had? I went for some engineering jobs but they didn't seem as nice as the one I'd had.

"But after a while, once I got involved with the customers and the people and the projects they were running, I found it more interesting. You saw a broad spectrum of the industry from high-tech to low-tech. I used to see engineers who'd say, 'Interesting, these transistors but we're sticking to valves.' One bloke I remember saying: 'I'll never get my head around transistors,' and I thought: 'Silly old buffer, that'll never happen to me.' But it has. Now, if I go and talk to a field applications engineer, he speaks a different language to me.

"I began to enjoy the job, particularly after my first taste of success. I had been to see an engineer who was interested in one of our transistors. I followed up and the guy got back and said they needed them in a hurry. I made special arrangements to get them over from the States quickly and got the order. Dennis mentioned it at the next sales meeting, calling it 'a nice piece of selling.' "

The next piece of success was when the sales manager resigned and Dick was called in and offered the job. "My first thought was: 'The sales manager gets a Zephyr.' " It was a crash course in learning how to manage people. He found that some of his salesmen relished his help and some didn't want him to interfere. Some liked him to go with them on customer visits, and some didn't. The key to doing his job was, he realised, seeing the differences between people and knowing who wanted help and who didn't. "Recognising these things is more useful than analysing figures."

He also learnt something more important: "If you possibly can, let others do it. If you've been doing something yourself, and you give it to other people to do, you'll find that half of them won't do it as well as you did it, but the other half will do it better than you did." That was an important lesson – although he didn't get a lot of time to put it into practice because Transitron was in a state of terminal decline by this stage. Although the UK subsidiary was doing all right, the US parent company was doing badly and the Americans dealt with the situation in their usual way – by firing the boss, repeatedly. When a new boss came over and criticised Dick's customer list for being too heavy on smaller companies, the writing was on the wall. "He asked 'Why do we have so many customers? I don't want to deal with small companies, I want to deal with big customers.' I said: 'We don't have products for big customers.' You don't usually get fired for incompetence but you do get fired for disagreeing with your boss. I left in January 1972 with £280 redundancy."

The month before he had been offered the chance of a distribution contract with the Florida semiconductor company

Harris. He had turned it down. Now it seemed like a lifeline. He rang them and they said: "Come over and talk.

"I bought the cheapest ticket I could get via New York and North Carolina and saw Harris. They did not want to commit to a one-man band. I came back devastated . . . well not devastated . . . disappointed."

In 1972, the semiconductor industry was in deep depression. There were few jobs open. Dick asked a company called LEMCO (London Electrical Manufacturing Company), which made low-tech capacitors, for a job and they said they would pay him commission if he sold any. "It was a real sweat-shop down in Hammersmith. That was hard because in this business you have to do a lot of work up-front before getting orders. I don't think I got any commission out of LEMCO at all."

He also did some trading on his own account, setting up a company called CNS Electronics, named after the initials of his three boys Christopher, Nicholas and Steven. Setting up a company got him thinking how little he knew about companies and how they worked and were structured. He started reading business books at this time which suggests the way his ambitions were beginning to take him.

CNS itself was a vehicle for trading and brokering deals, which was a tough thing to do without money. Luckily he found suppliers who would wait for payments until his customers paid him. "It was very precarious. I wouldn't like to do it now." A saving grace was the appointment of a new UK manager at Transitron. Dick offered to take the smaller customers off his hands in return for a commission on the sales he made to them. "I knew more about his account base than he did. And I knew where there were design-ins which were coming to fruition. So, in March 1972, the commission on what I had sold for Transitron was higher than the salary I had had when I was employed by them. It was the Transitron rep deal that kept me alive."

Still, it was an insecure lifestyle for a married man with three children. The next opportunity came from a chance meeting at a trade show with a couple of old friends who had just started a new distributorship called GDS and wanted someone to join them to run a subsidiary. "What I was doing was a lonely life and this seemed attractive. I got shares, a salary and a car. I was able to go back and get the Harris contract because I was no longer a one-man band."

The subsidiary of GDS Group which Dick ran was called GDS Marketing. It did well but he was increasingly worried by the way the group was being run. "As a subsidiary I was the last one to be serviced with any cash which gave me a problem paying Harris. I was uncomfortable with it."

For Dick, torn between loyalty to his friends and a sense that the business wasn't going anywhere, it was "the most traumatic time of my life."

As in previous crises, when he came close to the edge of disaster, circumstances came to his aid, this time in the shape of a Swiss businessman called Werner Stolz, inventor of a professional electronics machine called the Stolz PROM Programmer. He also had a business distributing high-tech components in Switzerland. "I had given him the Transitron line and helped him get his business going in Switzerland," says Dick. "Werner wanted to expand into the UK. He seemed to have lots of money – he always paid his bills on time." Dick went for it. Werner put up the cash and Dick got 51 per cent of the shares. Werner says: "I was happy with it because I wanted the company to succeed. Dick's risk was bigger than mine in giving up his job with GDS." Despite the risk, Dick had got what he wanted: "my own show."

After considering various names, they settled on Memec – an anagram which described what they were intending to sell – memory chips and other electronic components. His old employers were unhappy about his leaving and sued him under his employment contract which said that if he left he couldn't set up in a competing business. "There were quite a few sleepless nights – we had a young family, a mortgage, and I was being sued to stop me trading."

Dick's wife Carole had similar, though unexpressed, concerns. "Dick came back one night and said he thought he was going to do this. At that time we were living in a bungalow with three children and it seemed a bit of a flyer."

Now, looking back on the train of events which led to the formation of Memec, he says: "I'm a firm believer that things are circumstantial. If I'd been working for a good company I'd still be working for a good company. By now I'd be getting my gold watch from Texas Instruments. There's no logic to this."

An observer might say, however, that he had 'good jobs' at AEI and Associated Engineering, and gave them up to take a punt on the unknown and the risky, in search of something more. The observer might point to his character – as the youngest child he may have had more to prove; as a rebel he could have chafed in safe surroundings; as an independent mind he could have been seeking 'his own show'. Whichever it was, it was just as likely that his character sought risk, the unknown and opportunity as they pursued him.

For two years, the new company was on the edge. "We were not a well-funded start-up. For the first couple of years we were in survival mode," he says. "We ran the company from the bedroom of the bungalow," says Carole. "I typed all the invoices, boxed up the goods, took them to the post box and chased up the money." They learnt the key lessons of running a company early. "I realised I had to be able to make a profit and that I had to be able to collect the money," says Dick. "My overriding concerns were: are we going to be profitable this month? And: how are we going to pay the wages?"

He was sustained through many sleepless nights and worrying days by the belief that the underlying trend for the semiconductor industry was upwards. "I saw that here's a potential business with a relatively limited and focused product range which was going to grow, and if I could get the distribution right I would have a successful business."

Memec's business philosophy was based on another perception: "If you could get engineers to accept your product that was the basis of a good business. Now the reasons why engineers accept products can be strange. I have seen engineers accept a product because there's something sexy about it, or they like it because it's an elegant solution – even if there's a more cost-effective solution."

That emphasis on doing the up-front work to interest engineers in the product was a fundamental tenet from start-up to the present day. So what kept them going was operating in a growing industry, and believing that they understood the mind-sets of the people who ordered the product – design engineers.

Disaster soon struck. Once again, Dick was staring into the abyss. The whole of the first year's profit was wiped out when Memec's entire stock of microchips was stolen. They were not insured. Dick wanted to throw in the towel but Werner and Ed Sturmer, Memec's first employee, talked him out of it. "I told Dick we'd trade our way out of it," says Ed. Although, over time, Memec negotiated with the burglars and bought back the stolen product, times were tough. "It was very hard to make a living. We didn't have the volume," says Dick. The recognition of an opportunity at his old alma mater, Transitron – now in its death throes – went some way to solving the volume problem. Few other people would have recognised any opportunity there – in fact no one, except Dick, did. Asked why only he saw it, he replies: "necessity."

Transitron was generally seen as a dead duck. Twenty years before, the company had enjoyed heroic status as one of the first companies in the world to manufacture semiconductors and, in 1955, it became the world's second largest producer. Ten years later it was still in the world top ten producers. However, systematic 'milking' of the firm's profits, without reinvestment in new products, left it increasingly vulnerable and in the 1970s it was viewed as in irretrievable decline.

Dick saw an opportunity. "Transitron was losing money in the UK, sales were declining and costs were too high. I thought, if I can get the sole UK agency for their products they could close down their operation in the UK and save all that expense. I prepared a presentation and went over to the US. They went for it hook, line and sinker. There was quite a lot of residual business there – £1 million a year, if not £2 million – and it was a major fillip for us. For a while it was our No. 1 line in the UK."

From day-to-day seat-of-the-pants survival, Memec gradually took on momentum. "That was when I felt we could look a little more into the future. We asked customers what they were look-ing for, and would then go and find it." The employee count grew. Gradually, imperceptibly, the mood changed from a grim hanging-on to a feeling that the business would survive.

"I don't think I was convinced it was sustainable until I saw employees taking the initiative and running the model success-fully." Then came a turning point. "I began to relinquish responsibility and saw that the job was getting done without my direct involvement," he says. At that point, he first felt Memec was a success. "That's when the foundations of Memec were estab-lished. Responsibility had to be dispersed to a number of other people. We realised that we could build small business units around people and products. Responsibility had to be pushed down as far as possible because there is no other industry in which you have such a multiplicity of products, so many different customers, such sudden price changes, and such a rapid obso-lescence of product."

Ask Dick why he established the model of a series of autonomous operating units each with its own managing director and own product range, and he replies: "because I'm lazy and I'm a lousy manager." But you could also say that his view of the nature of the industry convinces him it is the best way to operate. Much depends on the people he chooses to run the businesses and on the mutual trust between them – their trust that he'll back them when needed, and his trust that he can leave them to get on with it.

"Everyone trusted Dick; it was the key to all his business success, it made it easy to develop the business," says Geoff Haynes, who ran Harris' business in the UK at the time Memec was founded. Dick's ability to pick good people is admired in the industry. Perhaps the best evidence of that is the many people who have left him to set up successful businesses of their own. As well as picking good people he was able to persuade them to join his company. Many recall being wooed into the Memec ranks over a meal or a session in a pub. They joined, it seems, because they liked him.

"Dick's a moral sort of guy, not in a stuffy sense, but he has a finely tuned feeling for what's right and what's wrong, and I think that's why people like him," says David Lathan, who was recruited in a pub in the very early days, then left Memec to manage one of the suppliers' businesses.

Once recruited, new people were given the chance to make their own way. "There was a great feeling of opportunity," says Ed Sturmer, the first person Dick took on at Memec. "We employed people as salesmen who in a few years were managing directors. Dick's good at leaving people to get on with it, giving them their head and supporting them. It was the making of me, personally. I turned from being a shy engineering type into a fairly confident sales and marketing guy, who became a managing director type."

Once a group had more than half a dozen product lines, the Memec business model recognised that it had reached the limit of its capability to satisfactorily handle the lines, and a new group would be set up. Memec's performance – out-growing the other big, global, distribution groups – suggests that its model works better than other models. "We were a success in business because we didn't know any better," says Dick. "If you don't know any better you'll go out and do something. You can think too much about a number of things, and in business there are many intangible and indeterminate things that you could continue to think about and never get an answer to. I have a firm belief that, if you don't know any better, you'll probably go out and do something. Not all the things you do will be right – and quite a few of them will be wrong – but there will be a few at least, that will be right."

Analysis can equal paralysis. "The Germans try to analyse everything to the third decimal place when there's only a 50 per cent probability of the thing happening at all," says Dick.

Success happened quickly for Memec. In their sixth year in business – 1980 – they had an offer of £1 million for the business. It set them thinking. After considering various options, they decided to sell 35 per cent of the company on the Stock Exchange and take the company public. The 35 per cent was valued by the market at £7 million. "So the offer of £1 million was not very good," says Dick drily. Memec's shares were oversubscribed by 58 times – a record in the City. Werner Stolz's original £7,000 investment was transformed into £2 million. Dick and Ed became multi-millionaires. Dick bought a BMW and a farm, Ed bought an aeroplane and a vineyard. Ed's mother, a staunch socialist, commented: "I don't agree with it but, while the system exists, I'm glad my son has exploited it."

Success allowed Dick to spend more time on his favourite sport – sailing. "The sailing I enjoy is competitive sailing. I'm not for going out and swanning around with a gin and tonic. It's serious stuff, over-the-side, cut-and-thrust stuff." The thrill of winning in both sailing and in business is, he says, "very similar."

For many years he has competed in, and more often than not won, the annual Three Peaks Race which involves sailing 380 miles and climbing for 32 miles up the three highest mountains in England, Scotland and Wales: Mount Snowdon, Scafell Pike and Ben Nevis.

In 1985 he won the Australian Flying 15 Championships at Waterloo Bay in Brisbane, Queensland, beating the world champions into second place. It was the first time in the 23-year history of the championships that a non-Australian had won the cup – the Cowes Slip trophy donated by the Duke of Edinburgh – and the Aussies unsportingly produced a deed of gift stating the cup could not be removed from Australia.

Dick explains the fascination: "Competitive sailing is very mentally intense. Tactics and being able to judge what is going to happen next are everything."

Despite his wealth, somehow life for Dick would never simply be all sailing and farming. Then, as now, the excitement of the deal was in his blood. "I have never been able to refuse an opportunity. I've been bound up in a very exciting, very competitive environment in which, if you didn't get there first, or if you didn't follow up, someone else would. When you've done it for thirty years it's very difficult to give it up."

The challenge after the 1981 public offer was to expand the business outside the UK since the trend of the industry was to go global. The opportunity the public offer gave him was to make it possible to use Memec's shares – now that they were quoted on the London Stock Exchange – as a currency with which to make acquisitions. The first attempt was a bit of a disaster. Memec bought a German company, Electronica of Hamburg. "It had no asset base, no good management. It was to be our entry into the German market but it didn't happen. I learnt that if you buy cheap it's often for a very good reason and can turn out to be expensive in the long run." A second German acquisition turned out to be little better.

Despite the disappointments, Dick felt he had to persist in trying to expand abroad. "I had this conviction that you had to be an international success," he says, adding the simple explanation, "the fax machine came in, you see."

With fax, global deals became instantly possible. Not to have been able to take orders, stock goods and supply them in a global environment would have become a severe impediment to growth. Expansions in France followed and were more successful than in Germany. Then, in 1985, came the most expensive gamble in the company's history – expansion into North America. "So many things happened because of opportunities which presented themselves," says Dick. He had been in the US and got a call from a friend who knew he was looking for a way into the American market. He wanted Dick to meet a young American who wanted to start up a business.

"Bob (Allison) was the most energetic guy I've ever come across," is how Dick describes the man he backed to get an American operation up and running. The problem was that the Americans wanted to expand quickly to get national coverage across the US without regard to profitability, while Dick needed to protect his share price in London in the face of mounting losses from the US – £100,000 in 1985, £300,000 in 1986, and £200,000 in 1987.

"Bob is a tremendous guy but he couldn't say no to anything. If there was a chance to open a new office, he would do it without ever thinking about the cost."

The friction caused Allison to resign three times. The third time, Dick accepted. "I had a number of approaches from people wanting to buy the business," he says, "but if I'd sold, the global vision would have been shattered." Once again loomed the threat of being downgraded from the A stream to the B stream.

Dick went to America himself, putting his reputation on the line. The Americans were expecting to hear they'd either been sold, or closed down, or substantially cut back. Instead, Dick told them that he had a global strategy for Memec, that you couldn't have a global strategy without a presence in the US, and that they were Memec's US presence.

The Americans were immensely relieved and cheered. Dick stayed for six months, by which time the US operation was in profit. A decade later Memec's US sales topped $1 billion.

In pursuit of the global strategy, Memec moved into Asia in 1988 – again the result of a recommendation from a friend leading to an acquisition. Other acquisitions followed. By 2000, Memec Asia had annual sales of $360 million.

Looking back, he rates these as his most satisfying achievements. "Seeing things grow in different continents – particularly the American and Asian situations – gave me the greatest pleasure, because so many people said I was crazy and sometimes I thought they were right."

In 1991 he made what he now acknowledges to be his greatest mistake. Fearing an assault on Europe by the expansionist US industry leaders Arrow and Avnet, he accepted an offer from the German industrial giant Veba to buy Memec for £75 million. He stayed on as chairman.

He realised it was a mistake when Memec subsequently out-performed the Americans. In 2000, Veba put its electronics interests up for sale and Dick worked with Schroder Ventures on a buy-out of Memec. Despite a counter-bid from Wall Street takeover specialists Kohlberg, Kravis and Roberts, the $760 million offer from Dick and Schroders succeeded.

Shroders kicked in another $260 million of capital to expand the group in a year when it was growing rapidly on the back of a worldwide semiconductor boom which saw Memec's sales top $3 billion. "There's never been a grand plan," insists Dick. "All there have been are opportunities."

Grand plan or not, he's been following some internal route map. Franklin and Tennyson had their influence, while the youngest child syndrome and the early shock of near-relegation to the B stream were powerful motivators. Sustaining him through the tough times were the early and abiding interest in things electrical and the certainty of their commercial potential.

Ask him his advice for people starting out, and he says: "There's no substitute for doing it, although sometimes you have to drive yourself to do it."

The most important lesson? "Delegate but never abdicate."

What drives him? "Fear of failure."

HANS SNOOK

H ans Snook is the founder and CEO of Orange, the mobile telecommunications network operator which, in 2000, was sold to France Telecom for £30 billion. Driven by a thirst for adventure and travel, he got caught up in the beginnings of the wireless phone boom in Hong Kong. Later he went to the UK where he set up Orange, one of the greatest success stories of the mobile revolution.

In his infancy, his father used to read *The Eagle* to him. He has never forgotten the interest in new ideas, and especially in new technological ideas, which the magazine triggered in his boyhood imagination. Later on, it was Arthur C. Clarke and philosophy that fed his voracious appetite for reading.

His early boyhood was spent in England. His parents – his father was English and his mother German – had met after the war in Germany where he was born. The family moved to England when he was two then, when he was eight, emigrated to Canada where he completed his secondary education and enrolled in university in British Columbia. "I kept switching subjects," he says. He tried economics, political science and philosophy, eventually doing his major in English Literature and his minor in psychology. He was not a conventional student. "I did not read any of the novels in my English literature class, and I never turned up to any of my psychology classes." He admits to being distracted in the sociable attractions of a nearby beach, and the companionability of the cafeteria.

An ingrained instinct to make a buck surfaced early and, in his last year of university, he worked the graveyard shift in a hotel. The combined effects of social life and holding down a job took their inevitable toll on his academic studies. Realising he had neglected his books, he decided to go to summer school to catch up on the credits he needed to graduate – but fate intervened.

A job as credit manager came up at the hotel. He applied for it, got it, and plans for summer school and graduation went out of the window.

Few people would give a job as a hotel credit manager priority over taking their degrees. That he did so stemmed from two aspects of his character – a longing for independence, and a susceptibility to the lure of adventure.

His time in England, when he'd seen his parents wait on a council house list, made him feel that he needed to be the master of his own fate. His view of life as being an adventure had been implanted by reading. That people could go out into the world and decide the course of their lives was something that books had convinced him was possible. Believing in it, he wanted to plough his own furrow.

There was also another factor in his decision – he loved the hotel business. He liked the twenty-four hour working of the business and the fact that it was all to do with people. "Lots of strange things happen with people – that part was fun," he says.

Typically, he was determined to be not a good credit manager, but a great credit manager. As soon as he started, the controller of the hotel had told him that his predecessor had been excellent in the job, and that he'd be doing really well if he performed even close to her standard. This fired him to do better than she had, and he worked for eight months secure in the knowledge that he'd outperformed this paragon. Then a new controller came in with quite different ideas. After questioning his performance targets, the following conversation took place:

"You've got these big piles of paper on your desk."

"I'm still trying to get to them."

"Pick them all up and throw them in the waste basket," said the controller. "Whatever's in that pile, if it's important, will come back to you. If it's not important, it will never come back to you. So forget about it."

It was advice which appealed to his free-thinking nature. Moreover, it turned out to be effective. Within a year, the hotel's credit management was judged to be the best in the entire group of 52 hotels. Years later it was advice he was to remember and implement when he was setting up the Orange network in the UK.

His success as credit manager led to promotion as assistant controller of the flagship Westin Hotel – the Bayshore Inn. This, in turn, led to Hans being requested to open a new hotel for the group as controller in Calgary. Having no desire to leave Vancouver, he quit to become controller of a smaller group of hotels based in that city. Subsequent to that, he was general manager of another large Vancouver hotel and opened a brand new hotel. He later left Vancouver and the hotel industry to pursue a love interest (who later became his wife) who was living in, of all places, Calgary. In Calgary, he became an estate agent, selling residential property, but eventually something in him made him rebel against having to persuade people to buy houses. Although successful, he didn't like many of the high-pressure sales techniques used in the real estate industry.

He then opened and managed a new hotel in Calgary before leaving to go back-packing: "the best decision of my life," he now says.

The housing market in Calgary was, at that time, in a deep depression. He actually owned two houses in the town, both of which were worth less than their mortgages. He sold them both for one dollar. With $15,000 in savings he set off to see the world.

He started his travels in Asia and, after six months, found himself in Hong Kong. There he was offered a job with a local paging and computer company called Young Generation. He told them he would give up his back-packing for one year and work for them.

He liked Hong Kong, which was full of hard-working people getting things done pragmatically and successfully. It suited his character. "At the end of the year they convinced me to stay on one more year." As the second year came to its close, he gave notice to end the tenancy on his apartment and prepared to hit the road. One week before he was due to set off, however, he got a call from an executive at Hutchison Whampoa. Over lunch he was offered the job of running Hutchison Whampoa's cellular and paging business. Interested, and aware of the job's potential, he agreed to give it a year. That was in 1986, and he could see the opportunity. The mobile communications business in Hong Kong was fragmented and disorganised. He realised that a unified network under one name, with one brand, could be hugely attractive to consumers. That's exactly what he accomplished.

A logo – four squares – was created and the company name Hutchison was adopted. He completely replaced its equipment, put in brand new computer systems, initiated a new customer service system, and started buying or renting retail properties in

Hong Kong. Without anyone finding out his plans, which could have affected existing business, he quietly renovated fifteen stores.

All fifteen were opened on the same day. "There was absolute consternation. I had everybody in uniform. It took off like a rocket but, funnily enough, the stores were blue, and people said: 'You can't use blue, it's the colour of death in Hong Kong.' But I thought: 'It's a new world, forget it. We'll put blue in because blue is our logo.' "

So successful was the launch that Hutchison became, at that time (1988–9) the most profitable cellular and paging company in the world.

There were some hiccups. One of them, as is usual in such projects, was that the computer system didn't work as it should have done. The other one was that, so keen were the staff to answer their phones, that they picked them up before callers heard a ring. This disconcerted customers so much that they couldn't collect their thoughts and tended to cut off their calls. The staff had to be told to let the phone ring fully – but only once – before they picked up the receiver.

The computer problems were solved by chance. One of the staff knew a young Australian who was about to take off on a back-packing tour of the world. It was suggested that they should try to get him to stop off in Hong Kong for a couple of months to have a look at the problems. "He turned out to be an incredibly hard worker. He stayed for three months, and things started to turn around. He understood the equipment and we started getting things fixed." After three months, the Australian was preparing to leave, to carry on his back-packing trip. He was persuaded to stay on for another three months. "We did this four times, and then we convinced him to actually come on board. He was 22 years old. His name was Richard Brennan, and today he's the commercial director at our group here in the UK. He's fantastic."

The back-packing trail was a regular recruitment agency for Hutchison. Graham Hill Howe, who became the Orange finance director, was also back-packing and ended up in Hong Kong working for Hutchison.

From Hong Kong, Hutchison expanded the business into South East Asia, first Australia, then Thailand, and then Malaysia. The company had great success in these countries but it was still troubled by one country where things were not running smoothly – the UK. Eventually Snook was asked to go over to the UK to analyse the problems and make recommendations.

That was in 1992. Hutchison had the Rabbit telepoint mobile business in the UK, were building a dedicated mobile data network, and had started on the PCN licence-building programme. Snook quickly identified that they had over-paid for the cellular reselling business, and that the paging business was struggling. It took him two months to make his recommendations, which were to close down the Rabbit business, stop the building of the dedicated mobile data network, write off about £280 million and invest another £700 million in PCN technology. "To their credit, and to my fear, they said OK. What I was afraid of was what they said next: 'Hans, since you recommended that, and we have accepted your recommendation, we need someone we can trust to implement it."

He went. For a time it was a bad experience – closing offices, laying people off and coping with a bad press. The latter problem he solved when he invited his worst critic, the London correspondent of the leading Hong Kong daily newspaper, The *South China Morning Post*, out to breakfast. Never, up to that time, a fan of the press, he steeled himself to the task and explained to the newspaperman exactly what he was trying to do. From that moment on, the tone of the journalist changed, and the articles became positive. The experience also changed the way he felt about journalists. From then on he respected the difficulties under which they work, and appreciated that most were trying to write an honest story.

After the cuts came the job of selecting a management team from within the company. People were identified: successfully, as it turned out, because most of them remain in the company management. The organisation was, at that time, subject to the 'warring tribes' syndrome. "That's why I needed good people who could transcend these things and help bring the different groups together."

He could see disaster looming for the new network. Although the engineering department told him they were building a great network, he found out for himself that it wasn't up to the standards he expected. He personally drove around the country, testing the signal strength and making calls on the new network. The moment of truth came when he went to a Marks & Spencer store in London. After failing to get a connection from inside the store, he called up his engineering department and the following conversation ensued:

"I can't make a call."

"Did you also try it outside?"

"Yes."

"Did you try it outside and, while you were on the call, walk into the building?"

"No."

"Oh well, if you did that you could keep the connection."

"So if I'm in M&S, and I want to make a call, I've got to go outside the building, make the call, and then walk back in the building?"

"Yes, that's right."

"You are absolutely crazy. Can you imagine what a customer would think?"

"Well, these things operate by the laws of physics."

"Engineers!" he says laughing.

Refusing to accept such a limitation on his network, he asked Hutchison for another £250 million to beef up the network's capabilities. He appreciated that the efficiency and integrity of the network was the bedrock on which the business rested. Refusing to compromise on the network's capability cost £250 million, and delayed the launch, but he had no doubt that it was the correct decision.

Critical to the success of the network was the choice of name, logo and advertising campaign. A massive process of elimination and analysis went into deciding on an orange square. "It seems silly," he says, "but it worked beautifully."

The launch advertising campaign has acquired the status of folklore, going down in the annals of the advertising industry as a classic. First came pure black posters with words on them like 'laugh', 'smile', and 'cry'. Nothing else. Then, after two weeks, a logo appeared in the corner. Finally came 'Orange'. Everybody was asking what it meant.

An old lesson from his Calgary days came in useful when he was presented with the market research that had been done for the new network. The researchers had been asking people what they wanted from the new network. He spotted that this was the wrong question, when customers could have no idea about the technology's capabilities, and that the right question was: 'What do people dislike about the current systems?'

He gave them the same advice about the research as the hotel controller had given him many years before: "Just throw it away."

Having found out what customers did not want in the new system, he set about adding features which the other networks did not have. Orange was the first mobile network to offer caller ID, to allow a split between personal and business billing, to permit per second charging and to operate a free answering service. Orange was also the first to come up with Over The Air Registration (OTAR). What that allowed customers to do was walk in to a shop, pick a phone, pay for it and go home. At home they could go through the material, decide what tariff they wanted to be on, plug the phone in and charge it up. Then, whichever button they pressed, they would be automatically connected with the Orange registration centre. A cheery welcome from the registration person would be accompanied by any advice they needed on how to choose a tariff.

Another innovation was to automatically link a customer's incoming call on an Orange phone with their account record, so their name would show up on the screen of the person taking the call and they could greet the customer by name.

"People were amazed. They'd say: 'How do you know it's me?' We were the first people to do it, and it went down fantastically well because people like to be greeted by name. That came out of my hotel industry experience. I knew that the more often you can call a guest by their name, the happier they are."

Initially, no High Street retailer would touch an Orange phone which, at £249 and £299, were the most expensive phones on the market. Orange made no concessions to the retailers, refusing to subsidise them. "There were times when it looked really bad," he recalls. "I told my people: 'If you are going to do something, don't be afraid to lose. Once you are afraid to lose, you are probably not going to win.' "

By sticking to their guns, public opinion gradually turned in Orange's favour. By the time of the launch, every single high street retailer was selling Orange – the first time any network operator had achieved 100 per cent coverage.

With the network up and running, and phones in the high street, the main focus now was on customer service. One key measure of customer satisfaction in the mobile phone business is churn rate – the percentage of customers ending their subscriptions. "Orange's churn rate is less than half the industry average in the UK and one of the lowest in the world," he says. "At the same time, the usage is higher in general than anybody else, hence our average revenue per customer is higher, not because we charge more, but because we give more services to people."

When it came to the pre-pay market, Orange did not tell people, as other operators did, that a pre-payment had to be used up in a certain period of time. And they did not include hidden charges in the pre-payment – they all went on airtime. That was highlighted to the public in an advertising campaign that said Orange had no 'ouch' in its voucher. It was followed by a campaign to promote flexible off-peak times, allowing customers to choose their own off-peak periods, which ran under the slogan: "There's no 'eak' in our off-peak."

His is a customer-related business philosophy: talking to them; understanding them; finding out what they don't like; fixing it; then seeing if there are products and services which can be added on.

Much importance is placed on the value of branding, which is something new to the mobile industry. "I don't think most companies really understand what a brand means," he says. "Our definition of brand is a promise delivered to customers."

In 1996, Orange went public and had the most successful mobile flotation in European history, with a value of £2.5 billion. Four years later, in November 2000, France Telecom bought the business for £30 billion. Between 1996 and 2000, Mannesman of Germany had bought Orange, and Vodafone of the UK had bought Mannesman. All the Orange shareholders over the years – Hutchison Whampoa, British Aerospace, Mannesman, and Vodafone – have done extremely well out of their investments. After being bought by Mannesman, Snook declined the offer of a seat on the board, preferring to be identified with his own show. To such a strong character, running his own show was important.

Then came the, initially friendly, but later hostile, bid for Mannesman by Vodafone. Snook provided Mannesman with much of the ammunition they needed in their fight – which was his fiduciary duty – but he thought that a victory for Vodafone would be no bad thing, because it was likely to result in a separate public listing, and independence, for Orange.

When Vodafone won, competition regulations required it to divest itself of Orange. France Telecom approached Vodafone in the summer of 2000 and, by the end of the month, had agreed a purchase price of £30 billion.

He has a visionary view of where the industry is going: "Our business in the future is not so much about mobile phones and communications, it's about giving people control over their world."

He sees the phone becoming a 'personal electronic servant', where the customer chooses the sex, voice, look and style of this servant, then gives it orders by speaking to it. For instance, if you want an air ticket to San Francisco, you'll tell it the day and time. It will already know your preferences on airline, class of ticket and seating. It will search the Web and come back with the options – neatly arranged in the order which your electronic servant thinks will suit you best.

Snook combines a vision of what the technology can deliver with a no-nonsense approach to execution. Common sense is the basic guideline for his business decisions. Trusting his own instinct is the way he validates those decisions and, he says: "if the decisions aren't working out the way they should be – bloody well find out why."

In November 2000 he announced that, in 2001, he would stand down as CEO of Orange to become special adviser to the chairman of France Telecom. Very few people have the ability to found, head up and run a business which creates £30 billion worth of shareholder value in eight years. In years to come, the Orange phenomenon will be looked back on as one of the classic success stories of the mobile age.

MALCOLM MILLER

Malcolm Miller is an unlikely digerati, having started off his career at Bird's Eye Foods. The high-tech world started to attract him when he saw the success of Amstrad. He asked for a job there and spent 16 years at the company. When Pace Micro Technology, which makes set-top boxes enabling digital TV, got into financial trouble, Malcolm was headhunted to save it. It looks as though he will.

"I've always been interested in mechanical things. When younger, I used to dismantle petrol-driven lawnmowers and carburettors just to see how they worked," says Malcolm.

How did he get interested in engineering? "I don't know. No one's ever asked me that question before. Meccano sets maybe."

His interest in business came from the family background. "My grandfather had a chain of bespoke tailors, though I never had any inclination to get involved." Nevertheless, the family's tailoring experience taught him a lesson – manage change or be changed. "They couldn't see that the ready-made revolution was happening. It overwhelmed them."

In 1976, after graduating, Malcolm went to Bird's Eye Foods. As a graduate, he did everything from statistical analysis to working in the factories to marketing and sales. Then he started showing symptoms of having caught the high-tech bug. "I'd heard about Amstrad – it was a small company then but it was doing lots of different things. In 1979 I went along, saw Alan, and thought: 'I can make my mark here.' I had something to offer because I understood marketing.

"I wanted something more exciting, more progressive, than food. Looking at a set of hi-fi components, and evaluating them, is more interesting than thinking how to re-form cherries and add syrup. I like a challenge, I like change and something new."

At Amstrad, he went from product manager to marketing manager, marketing director and then managing director. In 1994, after 15 years, he left to join Sega and became responsible for Sega Europe.

Why did he leave Amstrad for Sega? "If I hadn't moved then, I would have ended up an Amstrad-only person. I think wanting to be my own boss was the key thing."

Why did he want to be his own boss? "I think it's the best way in which you can explore ideas, and use experience, and develop products, people, concepts and strategic thinking."

He found the culture gap a problem. 'Working with the Japanese can be difficult for Europeans. There is caution but tremendous respect on both sides, particularly by the Japanese for Britain for its creativity, innovation and entrepreneurial spirit. However, creativity and entrepreneurial spirit can be unsettling for the Japanese who are steady, logical, methodical and don't like to be surprised.

"In some ways it was a superficial job because one could never get close to the Japanese. There is an inherent distrust. When I talked about rewards and bonuses they couldn't understand it. They can't reward people like we do or the Americans do. They thought their reward was in working for the company – the kudos.

"The Japanese, though, are very good at letting things lie – not killing a thing off. They will let things play themselves out and see if there is a opportunity to develop. They try not to burn bridges.

"So you tend to learn. You have to be careful because sometimes things are right at the wrong time. People say they've tried something and it didn't work, but sometimes there are opportunities that aren't right at the time. With Sega I learnt that some things are worth taking a second view on. An example of that occurred a year ago at Pace. We have an information appliances division working on internet appliances. People were saying: 'Standalone Internet boxes have been tried before, Hermann Hauser tried it four or five years ago.' Four or five years ago, Web browsing was interesting, e-mails were interesting – but they were for the enthusiasts who had PCs. So I was sceptical about this: Should we keep it?

"Before the Sega experience, I would have been very quick to make a harsh judgement. But colleagues said: 'It's a great team and has a valuable customer for the product' – that was Alba with their TVs – and, within the next three to six months, it was quite clear that there was a product, there was a customer, and now there is much more interest in it because Web browsing, Internet access, e-mailing from simple appliances is something which is in demand from conventional consumer companies and very much in demand from countries like Brazil and China."

Why did he leave Sega to join Pace? "I was on holiday in Marbella one weekend in June 1997 with friends, and a phone call came from a headhunter. They told me about a company which had lost one of its founders, and they were looking for a CEO. A lot of things got the better of me – curiosity, the feeling of challenge, an opportunity to turn something around. Also it was a great opportunity to create some wealth. The shares were at a very low price – about 50p."

Did he see it as an opportunity to make money for himself? "Yes. For me, and also for others in the company it has become an important driver, and I think it was an important driver for lots of the people in the company.

"One of my colleagues told me recently, 'The best thing we have done for company spirit and motivation is the widening of the share save and option schemes. It has made a big difference to attitude and diligence. It is true, in some ways, that we have created a group of people who have become intent on watching the company's share price, but they rightly believe that the company's value, and their wealth, are linked to the effort that they put in.

"It took from June to August to reach an agreement. I left Sega in September and joined Pace on November 17. There were mixed feelings in my family about it. This company was in Yorkshire and I had to spend a lot of time there. That was strange for the family – and a bit different for me – but you only come this way through your career once and, if there are opportunities, you have to go for them. No one knows how long one's going to be around."

Why did he go for a company that was in trouble? "Pace had the right kind of ingredients: it had problems, but it had some very bright people; it was very keen on product engineering, and product quality and reliability. The future was digital – I could see that digital TV was going to happen. Pace had stumbled while pay TV operators across the world delayed plans to roll out digital TV.

"I could see that the PC was not going to reach anything over 45 per cent penetration in the world. In Brazil and China it is much less. So I could see that TV was here for ever and I could see that digital TV was going to happen – BSkyB was starting to roll it out in some areas – and I could see that Pace was undervalued.

"In some ways the company didn't know itself what it was valued at because, when I arrived, expectations were of a profit of £10–12 million whereas the market thought it should be more like £20–30 million."

So almost his first job on arriving at Pace was to go and tell first the Pace board of directors, and then the City, that all their assumptions were wrong. "I had one advantage in that John Dyson, the new finance director, and I had discovered the true health and value of the company very quickly. Within six weeks we learnt that previous management had retained resources in areas that didn't need them, and was trying to increase profits and business where market potential didn't yet exist. Above all they were losing confidence in themselves.

"For some reason they were not close to the market volumes and direction. They also weren't sure where to establish the budget and what provisions had to be made.

"We had valuable discussions with the board on forecasting and general business management. There were issues to deal with but there were great opportunities.

"BSkyB was going to launch, and we were strongly favoured there because we had a very good relationship with them and our technical solution was good. OnDigital was going to launch as well. We had started to supply Canal Plus [the French digital broadcaster], we had business in Brazil and Mexico, and we had customers all over the world.

"It wasn't: 'Sorry chaps, it's all doom and gloom for the next year, and I don't know where our next product or customer is coming from.' It was: 'They haven't made provisions, there's bad debt, there's stock to write off, but we have some great relationships with some key and very large customers, products rolling out, and we have more business coming in throughout the next two years.' "

How did he get that across to the board? "By being very honest and up-front. If you have bad news, you come out with it; you don't try and hide it, you come out with it as fast as you can and you just say it to people."

Having briefed his board, he then had the even more daunting task of telling the City. "At Amstrad I had been to the City before to give them the numbers they expected, or to mould them into a new way of thinking about a project, but going to them and telling them that what they thought the company was going to achieve was not going to be achieved – that was not a very happy time, and it was not something I would like to repeat – ever.

"We knew that we only had one chance at this. You can only do this once. New guys can come in and say: 'Look, we've found something.' You couldn't go back six months later and say: 'Ah, I forgot about something else which I didn't tell you about.'

"When you first arrive at a company you take stock of your assets, resources and value. We felt we had a single chance to direct the company in this fast-moving and very exciting business. Many institutional shareholders gave us this chance, but some did not."

Why was he confident? "If you know you have a business, if you have customers and a product they want, then you feel much more comfortable. If people doubt you, or question you along that route, it doesn't put me off.

"I always say that the proof is the results, so the current ups and downs of technology stocks don't worry me too much. I know we have a strong future and customer relationships that will provide value to shareholders and employees and profitability.

You must be sure of that – and we question ourselves on everything. On every product we produce, every margin – we are our own greatest critical assessors. So every question anybody asks us, we've already answered it ourselves.

"We found out where the bottom was. That's very important. That's No. 1. You say: 'This is the bottom and this is where we can rise from.' We found out what was needed to succeed – where the business was going – and we had a lot of help, in that digital TV was about to take off. Things happened at the right time for us.

"I saw there was a basis of engineers, and what I had learnt at the time was that whereas trading companies have to keep spotting opportunities, engineering companies have engineering developments that create products for you in the future.

"I stand up and talk to all the staff every three months, and I say: 'It's down to you; we cannot do it without you. We work as a team, I cannot do it on my own. The executive team alone cannot do it.'

"I don't know how many believe it, but it's true. Everyone in the company forms the organisation so why shouldn't they enjoy profit-related schemes and the rise in share values?

"I feel that the US has created an unusual breed of people – a class of people who have become very wealthy, who go on to transfer their wealth to others and who go on and do other things.

"You see many people leave Microsoft to go and set up their own software companies around Seattle. I think this is something we need to do. We need to put back things into society to do with education, and structure, and wealth creation, so that it perpetuates itself."

The only way to do that is to let engineers get rich. Therefore rewards based on the share value of the company are particularly important to him. "It allows the company to be driven faster and better than any other scheme that anyone has ever come up with. What really drives people on is their own success, and the company's success, and sharing wealth. One might call it greed, but it does drive the company.

"If the people involved in the operation have shares in the company, then they can mutually succeed. If they see that meeting customer requirements within timescales, at the right margin levels and right price, equals more business, more profits, a higher share price, then their objectives and rewards are seen as the same thing. If you can complete that circle, you have a happy environment. But if you have an engineer who's not really associated with the customer, doesn't know what he wants, couldn't care whether he wants it or not, just gets his salary at the end of the year, so whether the profits go up or down it doesn't matter to him – then you haven't created that circle which gives you continued success. With a bit of good fortune I think you'll find that some of the people who've worked for our company, and other companies which have been hugely successful, will have created enough wealth to go off and start up their own thing. But for that to happen, first you have to allow them to create wealth."

After touching bottom and establishing a reward structure, the next step was to ensure competitiveness. "We have strict policies about the cost of products, the margins, how fast we get management accounts. We know we have to get down to the lowest cost ahead of competition.

"In the electronics business we're all trying to find the solution, we're all trying to get there before anyone else. It's a big race, and we are trying to give value to the consumer and value to the shareholder. It's a relentless process, and a very fast process.

"The worst thing you can do is get caught at any stage. In one way it's like the PC business – if you get caught with the wrong processor, or the wrong hard drive, you're finished. You do not get a second chance. What we do is interpret the digital solution for the broadcasters' needs for the benefit of the consumer, and we develop that in the fastest possible way, at the lowest possible cost. We are not as involved in distribution as the PC people. Development is more important for us because being first in the market means everything."

He also had to set financial goals. "We laid out a model which it would be difficult for others to pursue. We decided we were going to be very competitive. We would live with 20 per cent margin, 15 per cent operating costs, 5 per cent profit before tax. As it turned out, the first year was better than planned: 8 per cent profit with a margin of 26 per cent. During our second year as a team the model reverted to the original model of 20 per cent margin, partly because of rising component costs. But because revenues were driving forward faster than operating costs, profits were held at close to 8 per cent."

What's he like in a crisis? "Every company faces problems. Trying to legislate for them is impossible. What can be changed is the way in which you tackle them. We face a mini-crisis every weekend. Don't ask me why, but it always happens on a Friday evening. It's how you approach it that's important. I've learnt a lot about crisis management – to be absolutely up-front about it and not hide from it."

Having sorted out the internal issues, he started to look outside Pace and aimed at becoming the chief tub-thumper for digital TV. "Our business could only grow as fast as the rate which broadcasters roll out digital services. So we've spoken for the industry about the value of digital TV, and interactive services, and Internet access. Wherever possible, we talk at conferences, and give views, and present reports which explain that there is a future in digital TV services.

"We've been helped a lot in that a number of very large companies have come along and said: 'Well, this looks like an interesting industry, we want to play in it as well.' Companies such as AT&T, AOL, Microsoft and many others. They're saying: 'We're not just going to receive these services and information over PCs or over Smartphones – TV is a great space to operate in.' They have added to the fuel which has been driving digital TV.

"On top of that, we have governments around the world saying: 'Analogue is going to be switched off, this broad spectrum is going to be sold off and it's going to be highly valuable – as we have already seen – so let's get onto digital very fast.'

"You will have seen us campaigning against anything which stands in the way of digital. We've taken it upon ourselves to be the spokespeople. We've been seen as representative because we have sat in the middle. We're not a broadcaster, we're not an operating system provider or a content developer. We're a platform provider and integrator."

What are his objectives? "To be No. 1 worldwide."

"It's a pretty hard target, but it has determined the volumes that have to be sold to customers. It is a great driver and there is no reason why we can't do it. Look at all the other people in the sector. They really are no different to us. We have got the advantage of focus – set-top boxes are the only thing we do – and focus is very important in today's environment.

"There's nothing special or magical about our competitors. They have got something in their favour – they're very strong in the US – but Thomson is actually a French company and GI is No. 1 because of its relationships.

"So let's go and get the relationships. We have the technology – we are ahead of them in technology because we focus on the box, whereas they have to roll out all sorts of different products."

What are the barriers to succeeding in the US? "Relationships."

How do you build them? "Take on people from the cable industry. We've just recruited a non-executive who has worked in the US cable industry for forty years. He worked for one of the largest cable companies. He knows everything, and I said to him: 'Why on earth do you want to do this? Do you realise we're a British company coming to compete in the US against US suppliers?' He said, 'That's fine, that's OK.'

"You have to learn that you can't do everything. You need help. So we've asked Cisco for help, and Microsoft for support, and they've been brilliant at helping us form relationships.

"A lot of British companies falter in the US. It's been a graveyard. They've had difficulty because they've taken on distribution and retail. We will form relationships directly with network operators and form strategic partnerships with others when retail becomes more important. We need more of those relationships and the potential is enormous. The forecast is that over the next four years 60 million cable boxes will be sold. There are 65 million homes in the US; 5 million have already got them, and they say the other 60 million will move from analogue to digital over the next four years."

Is the strategy succeeding? "I'm not successful yet. We have successfully managed the transition from a company that wasn't highly valued to a company that is moderately valued, but we haven't yet reached where we want to get to.

"We have successfully conveyed to customers our existing potential – that we have technology – and we have started to convince the wider shareholder base that we are a technology company, not just a builder of boxes from parts which are bought in, and we have successfully built confidence. But we're by no means successful. We still have a hell of a long way to go. The engineers, who some say I'm in love with, have created a huge amount for the company in terms of its image and achievement, but they still have a lot more to do."

How does he, a non-engineer, motivate engineers? "I once asked a headhunter the secret of success of today's CEO and she said to me, 'It's having a vision, being able to articulate it and knowing what you're good at and not good at.'

"When it comes to knowing what I'm good at and not good at – I'm not good at understanding the real cutting edge of technology, and I rely on people. The skill lies in trying to select the best people to manage the engineers. But I know what goes in at one end, and I know what has to come out the other end, and if we get it going in and coming out as fast as possible, we're going to have our product out on the market with a better performance, a lower cost, and the customers will be pleased.

"It's damn difficult finding the best people. I couldn't interview an engineer and tell you if he was any good. I rely on people to do that, and to drive the process, but they're driven by me."

How does he know they're doing the right job? "Because of the products that come out, and how they come out, and how they perform. By benchmarking us against the competition in terms of performance – qualitative and quantitative – timing and cost."

How does he lead? "You have to be out in front – to take the hit from the City, the customer or the employee who wants to complain. Being a leader comes from understanding the detail. It's great to delegate, but it's good to remember things, to pick up things which you use in analysis and conversation. To be a leader you have to know a lot of detail without getting bogged down by it."

Who does he admire? "Henry Nicholas, CEO of Broadcom. He works like crazy, is a great engineer, he knows all the detail, he's their greatest salesman, he has a very good team of people and he's very bullish about the future.

"Broadcom has very aggressive stock option plans. They've all done very well – not just from one product or idea; they're always expanding and adding new things. Broadcom is a great example of wealth creation."

Are all the engineers motivated by the stock option scheme? "People come in, they see others doing well, they see paths to promotion and reward. You can walk into companies which are giants but they feel dead. You walk into our office and there's activity, interest, enthusiasm, people who are excited about what they do and talking about things which are possible for the future.

"You have to have the right package. You have to have management, vision, selling ability – you can't just get a bunch of engineers and set them off down any path. It's got to be the right path in the right sector that's moving upwards.

"Digital TV's our path. Getting the right silicon and operating systems and the right engineers to make it work. Individually I go and see customers and go and see our teams to see if they're on track to deliver the product along the schedule. I don't wait till the thirteenth month and then say: 'Did you do it?' But I look at it in the third, fifth, seventh months and ask: 'How are we doing? And give it to me straight. Don't bullshit me, because it only gets found out in the end. And involve me. Tell me. A problem shared is much better than sitting on it and letting it fester.'

"I believe that the greatest companies in the world are pulling away from the rest. Technology means speed, inventiveness, deploying the right people, speed of delivery.

"I spend a lot of time talking to people, appraising performance and objectives, making sure we're approaching the right people and advertising in the right places.

"It's a question of understanding what the customer wants. Listening very carefully. Asking yourself: 'What does this customer really want?' If you sit there talking all the time you'll never find out.

"You have to ask yourself: 'What can I use to win that customer over to us?' Obviously there's a competitor against us. You ask, 'Who are they?' 'What can't they do that we can do?' 'Where are they better?' And we appraise their products. We ask, 'Where can we improve our features?'

"I'll phone customers up and ask them, 'What do we need to do?' And they'll say, 'well you should address this or that problem.' And we'll get on to that. It's being very honest with yourself. If we can prove to the customer that we're going to address problems, it's more important than having a visionary lead."

How does he find the first signs of success? "Very exhilarating. Winning is everything to everybody. I do take issue over the Labour party's view that musical chairs should be banned from school because it brings out the worst in people. If you're going to have a successful society there's got to be winners and losers. There's no winning without losing.

"Changing the company from being just a box-shifter to a technology company, and winning cable business as well as digital terrestrial businesss – doing that made people think: 'Hey, these boys aren't just a satellite company.' It showed that we could deliver different solutions to different customers. Winning customers gives everyone a great boost."

Like many others, he feels that the UK has been bad at high-tech manufacturing. "Traditional English manufacturing com-panies fear that step into the unknown. That step into that thing called technology. It's doing something different.

"It's a bit like watching older people use electronics. They're so scared of touching it. They think it's mechanical, and of course it's not. They think it will break, but of course it won't. It's like watching them trying to programme a video. They're thinking: 'I shouldn't really touch it.'

"When I look at British businesses I feel that they're all reluctant to say: 'I can be No. 1,' reluctant to step into that void that has mystery and danger in it, requiring new skills, new thought processes. Americans aren't like that. They boldly walk in, say; 'We'll turn this around,' they'll put investment in, shout about it from the highest building in New York – they'll just get on and do it, and the Japanese think they can refine and improve anything which anyone else does."

What does he see as the biggest single mistake UK industry has made? "Not appreciating the need for constant improvement. We didn't realise we needed to improve. We thought we'd made the best fax machine and the best word processor – there was no need to improve it."

What would he say to Gordon Brown or Tony Blair? "What they would love to have is a technological society, a digital society, a society that has access to information We should encourage the lead we have in the race to digitise British TV, and interactive services, and lead the world. Here we've got some momentum, here we've got a platform, here we've got British companies competing for content, for subscribers. If we can get momentum going behind that, and encourage those people to go and deploy those skills for other operations around the world, then we're going to have a much more successful econ-omy. You're only going to do that if you allow people to succeed. And success must mean that they personally enjoy greater wealth.

"I think Blair and Brown may secretly understand that, but I think they may see it as unpalatable. It may be seen as the musical chairs syndrome.

"I think the UK can succeed. I want to encourage that, but we're not very good at it. We ridicule success. I think we've got to get out of that trap. It will take some time. It has a lot to do with the media – like lastminute.com – you do get laughed at for failure in the UK, which you don't in the US."

What is the most important thing he does? "Motivating others."

How? "By giving them the right information and giving them a desire to succeed. I think human beings are all similar. Everyone likes success. Some people push themselves further than others, but everyone wants to hear: 'Well done.' Everybody wants to catch the bus, wants to win a prize, that's part of our life – of our nature – even a dog wants a pat.

"If you look at great companies, they're driven by successful people, who have successful people reporting to them, who want to take the company onto another level."

What are his skills? "Having vision, articulating it and delegating – because there's a lot I can't do; a lot I don't understand."

How important is it that people enjoy themselves? "Hugely. It's difficult to ensure everyone's enjoying life – I'm sure for some it's tedium and boredom – but if you can get the majority enjoying things, that's pretty good. It's interesting, because often that sense of fun and enjoyment comes out of winning and losing. You don't know when you've won until you're close to losing. You don't know what pain is until you've actually seen success."

What is his role? "I have to provide input and information all the way along. Plenty of information; plenty of feedback – what's right, what's wrong, what's succeeding, what's failing; plenty of participation, plenty of knowledge – my school motto was 'Knowledge conquers all.' It's probably true – if you've got the information you can deal with it; if you live in a vacuum, God knows what's going right and what's going wrong.

"I'm not the sort of person who can walk around saying: 'Hello. How are you? Have a nice day.' It's not in my personality – I can't do it. What I can do is talk to everyone *en masse* or to the managers.

"You have to get people on your side. You have to be humble too. If you don't know the answer, say so. If you're upset, say so. But do it in a constructive way. Don't make people lose their self-respect – it doesn't make for an enjoyable or happy person or company.

"I think successful business leaders are an unusual breed and you get the best and the worst from them. When I meet some successful people, I think: 'How can they be so successful and appear so nice at the same time?' With others I think: 'How can they be so successful and be such a pig all the time?'

"I don't think you can be an all-loving, wonderful person, sympathetic to everything and be hugely successful. You have to be tough at times. You have to do it in the best possible way. Getting one person in front of ten others and making them feel small is not a clever or constructive thing to do."

What advice would he have for a newly graduated engineer? "Come and work for Pace. It offers fantastic opportunities to express yourself, learn a lot and be a part of a winning team."

How does the job affect his family life? "I think, sometimes, some of the family think I expect great things from them – greater than they can deliver. I have to be careful not to take that attitude home with me. Home is not an environment like business. I can't say: 'Do that now,' 'Do that then.' You can't treat your family that way. I think the family's perception of themselves is: 'Do we have to live in his shadow?' I think they feel they might have to. Especially my wife: 'Is she a person in her own right or just Malcolm Miller's wife?' She certainly doesn't like being the latter. She needs her identity, self-respect, being important. That's part of family life – the wife looks after the home and the kids, and allows the husband to go out into the world.

"The kids, if you're not careful, can feel there's this almighty father figure that they can't live up to – or wouldn't want to – so they rebel and become difficult. I think my son wants to be hugely successful – without doing the bit between where he is now and where he wants to be – and my daughter wants to be fiercely independent.

"I think you do lose something along the way. It's very, very difficult to be this guy who wants to go and do all these things across the world and have an easy, complete, successful home and social life – never flare up at anything, never lose your temper, always understanding and always there when needed. It just doesn't work like that.

"I don't think there's a way round it. You're at a meeting. One of the guys gets a phone call and says: 'I can't make the flight to Tokyo. I know it's an important meeting. The wife needs me at home. One of the kids is ill.' You have to make some choices. I've told my wife: 'I can't be the nine to five guy. I've made this decision. I hope you'll support it. I'll have to make compromises. There are some rewards along the way – I hope.'"

Three years after he took over, Pace shares had gone up sixteen times. It looks as if his hopes may be realised.

THEMATIC INDEX